Million Dollar CEO Warrior Insights

Series 1

MIKE AGUGLIARO

With insights from: Brian Tracy, Cameron Herold, Mike Michalowicz, Larry Winget, and Dan Kuschell

ISBN-13: 978-1541188327
ISBN-10: 1541188322

DEDICATION

This book is dedicated to my friends who shared their insight with me – Brian Tracy, Cameron Herold, Mike Michalowicz, Larry Winget, and Dan Kuschell. Your contributions to life and business are profoundly invaluable.

CONTENTS

Action Steps: How To Get The Most Out Of This Book — p.7

Finding Giants — p.9

Read This Disclaimer — p.11

Conversation With Brian Tracy: Why Small Companies Need A Great Business Plan — p.13

Conversation With Cameron Herold: What Entrepreneurs Should Be Thinking About — p.43

Conversation With Mike Michalowicz: Why Entrepreneurs Should Take Their Profit First — p.75

Conversation With Larry Winget: Why People Aren't Getting The Level Of Success They Want — p.107

Conversation With Dan Kuschell: Grow Your Business And Maintain A Balanced Life — p.137

Bonus Insight: Breaking Down Limiting Beliefs — p.169

Special Report: Networking Your Way To Broke — p.173

ACTION STEPS: HOW TO GET THE MOST OUT OF THIS BOOK

You're reading this book because you want to grow your service business. But reading is only part of the process. I want you to be inspired and fully engaged throughout the process of business growth so I've listed several steps for you below. Think of it as an entry-level curriculum to grow your service business. Be sure to complete every step because they all work together.

1. **Read this book**. Actively read this book with a pen and highlighter in hand and a pad of paper and sticky notes nearby. Underline key points; add a star or exclamation point in the margin when you want something to stand out to you. On the pad of paper, make a list of the actions you'll take.

2. **Complete the action steps**. Throughout this book I've included sections called "Take Action!" Watch for these and when you get to them, complete each action step. Do them immediately.

3. **Bookmark CEOWARRIOR.com**: you'll find a wealth of resources to help you, including a blog, my upcoming events, and videos.

4. **Sign up for the newsletter at CEOWARRIOR.com**: this is a must-read newsletter that arrives in your email inbox weekly and you can sign up for it on the website above.

5. **Connect with me on social media**: Visit **CEOWARRIOR.com** to find all the social media channels we can connect on.

6. **Watch for my next Warrior Fast Track Academy**: Warrior Fast Track Academy is a 4-day event to help service business owners achieve real change and real success in their business. Make it a priority it attend! Learn more at **WarriorFastTrackAcademy.com**.

FINDING GIANTS

"I can't do this anymore."

That's what my business partner, Rob, said to me just over 12 years ago. We were both burning out and he was the first to put words to how we were feeling. We nearly shut the business down.

We didn't, of course, and we ultimately grew our home service business Gold Medal Service into the number one home service company in New Jersey. We went from two electricians and two helpers in two rusty vans... to 190+ people on our team. We went from a few hundred customers... to 125,000 customers. We went from struggling... to making more than $30 million a year. And just recently we completed the next phase of our business plan and sold the company so we can focus on CEO Warrior.

It wasn't luck that helped us turn things around. It wasn't a family fortune that paid our bills. It wasn't a magic wand. It wasn't a lucky lottery win. I didn't invent something.

Want to know what it really was? Actually, Isaac Newton said it perfectly, "If I have seen further than others, it is by standing upon the shoulders of giants."

When Newton said that, he was talking about his ability to achieve great advancements because he built on top of what others already achieved.

If you want success in business, don't reinvent the wheel. Find the giants, stand on their shoulders, and see further. In other words: LEARN and ACT, then do it again.

Gold Medal Service grew because I went out and found the giants and stood on their shoulders.

CEO Warrior does the same thing – it's growing because I found more giants and am standing on their shoulders.

And all the lessons I'm learning? I'm honored to be a giant on whose shoulders other business owners from around the world are standing on.

The quest of finding giants is never over. That's why I have a podcast where I regularly interview experts – so I can learn and so my listeners can learn. In this book, you'll find a collection of conversations with business experts on whose shoulders you can stand to grow your business.

Get a pen, highlighter, and pad of paper. Get ready to make notes. You will find millions of dollars of business- and life-changing wisdom in these pages.

READ THIS DISCLAIMER

The book you're about to read is a collection of conversations I've had with experts. It's important to note: These are ***conversations***, and people speak very differently than they write.

I could have had these conversations dramatically edited into a different form but they'd lose something in the process – they'd lose the raw, real, and "right now" feeling that conversations have. And, there's something about that rawness that add can add value to your understanding.

However, I have had these conversations edited slightly (in circumstances where the audio couldn't be transcribed for whatever reason or where an error was spoken) but for the most part, these are conversations themselves and you're invited to listen like a fly on the wall to the wisdom that is shared.

Why am I telling you this? One simple reason: Warriors learn wherever and whenever they can, from any source possible. If the conversational delivery method of these lessons bothers you, and you can't see past it to get to the lessons, then you may always struggle until you open your mind to the lessons that are everywhere.

You can also follow along with the conversations in audio by going to the link I provide at the beginning of each chapter. You'll find the audio, show notes (which I've also summarized in this book) and additional links and resources.

CONVERSATION WITH BRIAN TRACY

WHY SMALL COMPANIES NEED A GREAT BUSINESS PLAN

CEOWARRIOR.com/podcast-brian-tracy/

In this episode of the CEO Warrior Podcast, Mike Agugliaro interviews Brian Tracy. Brian is the chairman and CEO of Brian Tracy International, a company specializing in training executives and individuals for success. Brain is an author, keynote speaker, teacher, and so much more.

Main Questions Asked:
- What do you see as the problem in small companies today?
- Do great leaders create great culture?
- How should we develop better leaders?
- What would you say to someone who thinks they don't have enough time?
- What do you think business owners should pay attention to over the next few years?
- Can you share some wisdom around hiring and recruiting?

Mike Agugliaro:	Hello everybody and welcome to the CEO Warrior show. My name is Mike Agugliaro and this is a show dedicated to business owners, teaching you how to fast track your business growth and give you practical, doable tips that you can implement today, so grab your pen and notepad and let's get started.

Now today I'll be interviewing Brian Tracy about business mastery and business development. I'm so excited to bring him on, but let me tell you a little bit about Brian, if you don't already know who he is. Brian Tracy is the chairmen and CEO of Brian Tracy International, the company specializing in the training and development of individuals, executives, and organizations. He is among the top speakers, trainers, coaches, and seminar leaders in the world today. Brian Tracy has consulted for more than a thousand companies and addressed more than five million people in five thousand talks and seminars through the US, Canada, and 76 other countries worldwide. As a popular keynote speaker and seminar leader, he's addressed more than 250,000 people each year. Brian has studied, researched, written, and spoken for 35 years in the field of economic history, business, philosophy, psychology.

He's one of the top selling authors of 80 books that have been translated into 42 languages. Brian has written and produced more than a thousand audio and video learning programs, including the world wide bestselling *Psychology of Achievement* which has been translated into 28 languages. He speaks to corporate and public audiences in subjects of personal and professional development, including the executives and staff of many of America's and world's largest corporations. He's traveled and worked in over 120 countries on six continents and speaks four languages. Brian's also happily married and has children.

I've got to tell you, it is such an honor. How are you today Brian?

Brian Tracy:	I'm just great, thank you very much. How are you?
Mike Agugliaro:	I'm doing amazing, and Brian I've got to tell you I think the program (and tell me if I'm right or wrong about this), *Psychology of Achievement*, I think the first time I listened to it was on a cassette tape. Is that true?
Brian Tracy:	That's correct. It became the bestselling program on success in the world in, as you say, 28 languages.
Mike Agugliaro:	Yeah, that's amazing. You know what? I'd like to jump right into some subjects here so we make sure the listeners on this show get massive value. So everybody should make sure they've got pen and paper because every time I talk to Brian he delivers such great value.
	What do you see in small businesses, today, Brian? And specifically let's talk about business mastery and business development. What do you see as the big issues going on in small companies today?
Brian Tracy:	Well, the major issue is that they're spending too much time online and not enough time actually selling their products. There's a saying that says, "Online networking is actually not working." Many people think that if they send out email messages they're going to sell their products, and it doesn't always work because today we have to get right back to basics. The reasons that businesses are successful is because of high sales. The reasons they are unsuccessful is because of low sales, and everything else is commentary, and everyone does everything they possibly can to avoid getting out face to face with a customer and asking them to buy the product.
Mike Agugliaro:	Yeah. As good as the electronic world is, do you feel a lot of this is creating disconnectedness between the way people communicate compared to the past? I just remember my dad, you know: He was all about, "let's sit down, have a cup of coffee, and talk about a deal," and today people are trying to just close a deal over texting.

Brian Tracy: Yeah. Well, there's lots and lots and lots and lots of research on this. This is not an unexplored area. The fact is that you have what you might call a barbell in marketing today. It used to be that you had a bell curve where you had small esoteric products on either end and the massive products in the center. Today on one end you have what are called transactional products like a book on Amazon. If somebody tells you about a book then you go to Amazon and buy it; you're on and off in 30 seconds, and the book is there the next day. That's a transaction. That's what the internet is perfect for. We go all the way to the other end of the barbell and those are personalized, customized, tailored products that are special for each person, like a person in a restaurant ordering dinner for several people. You may have the same menu but people are going to order different dishes and different combinations and in different orders. These type of sales, customized, tailored sales, require face to face interaction with someone who asks questions, listens carefully, and tailors the product for you. Most people think that they can sell the tailored product, which is almost like a personal medical appointment, the same way they sell a transactional product online, and that's what causing a lot of confusion.

Mike Agugliaro: Yeah. I can see that. When you go in and you're talking, to companies today and you bring them back to the foundational pieces, like "Hey guys and gals, you need to think or consider doing this" what do you tell them?

Brian Tracy: Well, I put them through a process. As a matter of fact, I was just talking to one of my clients in Switzerland on this. I put them through a process called the Two Day MBA, Total Business Mastery, and what it does is it takes them through what I call the ten greats. I can it, "Build a Great Business."

The first great is great leadership. That means that you have to have someone who is in charge that thinks through clearly what needs to be done and then takes responsibility for doing it. The very best definition of leadership, and I've written 20 books on the subject, is person who accepts responsibility for results. They don't pawn it off, they don't hope other people will do it, they don't wish and pray and send out ads and buy lists. They take complete responsibility for results, so we explain the key qualities of leadership as identified over the years.

The second part is to have a great product, and here's the discovery, 90% of business success is determined by the quality of the product in the first place. Everything else is commentary. They interviewed the owners of what they call the Inc 500, the 500 fastest growing companies. This year the company that grew the most grew 68,000% in three years, 6,800 times in three years. Many other companies grew 100, 200, 300 times in three years. They asked them "If you had a million dollars to spend to increase your business, how would you spend it?" They all said "Improve the quality of the product." Spend every penny possible improving the quality of the product because if you have a high quality product, like an Apple iPhone, you can charge more money, you sell more, sell easier, make higher profits, and have greater customer satisfaction. If your products are in the bottom 80 to 90% then the only way that you can sell them against competition is by cutting your price, so therefore the only way that you can become free of price cutting and price wars is by having a really high quality product that people really and need and are willing to pay for.

That's 90% of business success, and it's astonishing how many companies that actually suffer, struggle, eventually go broke, never heard that before. They thought "well, I'll just find a real gimmick to sell it, I'll discount the price, I'll throw in an extra this and an extra that, and so on." No, no, increase the quality the quality of your product. You find that companies like Apple, they never reduce their prices. Also they do very little advertising because – why? – because everybody knows that they're the highest quality. If you want it, you just go and buy it, and you just pay whatever they ask, and they keep raising their prices. Their competitors charge half the price for a phone that many people say, like Samsung's, is almost as good, but Samsung is always cutting its price and cutting deals to get sales.

The third thing that we talk about is having a great business plan, and a great business plan is basically having goals for a business just like you have goals for your own personal life and you write them all out and you think through and you get accurate information and you make proper decisions and you take action on those decisions.

You take those three, great leadership, great products, and a great business plan, and you'll find that 80 to 90% of small and medium sized businesses don't have any of those.

Mike Agugliaro:	Yeah, I can see how important those are, and especially how it goes right in order. Question, Brian: do great leaders create a great culture or how does that play on that part?
Brian Tracy:	Peter Drucker, who I studied for years, said that "There may be natural born leaders, but there are so few of them that they make no difference in the great scheme of things." He said "Leaders are developed and almost always self-developed." Companies are very aware of this. Companies spend more money on management and leadership training than on all other training products and programs put together, because they recognize that leaders can be developed. I have trained more than probably a million managers, leaders, entrepreneurs, business owners over the years, and the people who come to my training are very often just starting off or just getting going, and they come back five years later and they're millionaires and multi-millionaires and they carry around my workbooks like Bibles and they constantly refer to key points – how do you hire? how do you delegate? how do you supervise? how do manage? how do you measure? how do you motivate? how do you plan? how do you market? how do you sell? how do borrow or raise money and funds? These are all specific skills that leaders have to learn, and the big companies

18

teach their managers this all the time.

Unfortunately so many small and medium sized businesses have what they think is a great product and what they think is a great market, often with very little validation, so that's it and they don't bother to learn the other skills.

Here's an interesting discovery. The first richest man in the world, at one time, now the fourth, just passed by Jeff Bezos, is Warren Buffet. Warren Buffet reads 80% of everyday, comes into the office, never checks email, never goes on Facebook, refuses to take phone calls. He puts his head down and he studies his business 80% of the time, so does Charlie Munger who's his personal advisor; they've been together for 30 years. Carlos Slim, sixth richest man in the world, reads and studies his craft, his business… well it's 60 to 70% of the time every single day.

Then you look at people who are trying to make businesses successful, they don't do anything. They play on the internet. They send Facebook messages, and they wonder why the sales aren't coming in, so what I do is I teach people methodically; that this is not a miracle. There's over three million businesses in the United States, there's very specific reasons why they succeed or why they fail, and if you do what other businesses do to succeed, then you'll soon get exactly the same results, and if you don't, you won't. People who go to my seminars, they're just shaking their head, they say "I can't believe I've never heard of this stuff before. Nobody ever told me this." They go out and they apply it and they transform their businesses. It's almost like a 100% hit rate. It's just absolutely amazing and very satisfying for me. I've taken businesses that were on the verge of bankruptcy and after they have been through my course they turn the business around in 30 days, and they come back and they say "You know, you saved my life. You saved the jobs of 42 people. You saved my parents' retirement. I never knew this stuff before and now I know it." Anyway, that's what I do, and that's what gives me my greatest satisfaction.

Mike
Agugliaro:

Yeah, I love that. That's so rewarding to hear how you're changing so many lives with that information. Let's dig a little deeper into how leaders are developed: so if you were to give us three or four action items that if we had somebody in our company that we wanted to develop to be better leaders, what would you tell us are some action steps that we should consider?

Brian Tracy:

Well, leadership as I said is accepting responsibility for results, so I've done 150,000 hours of reading over the last 50 years. I have read 6,000 book. I took 4,000 hours at the university in an MBA program, so I know an little bit about the subject, and as I said I published 20 books on leadership by some of the biggest publishers in the world, and so the first thing you ask is, the first job of a leader is to set and achieve business goals. It's the number one reason for leadership success, and so the most important word first of all is clarity. Be absolutely clear about the most important goals, never more than two or three, usually just one, that you can set and achieve.

I just completed one of the most exhaustive studies on business success, 22 countries, 25,000 business, 150 researchers, 12 years of research, and they found that there's three critical factors, three plus one for a successful business worldwide, and for successful countries worldwide. Number one is clear goals and objectives, is the company is absolutely clear about what it wants to accomplish and every single person is absolutely clear about their goals and their objectives as well, and the whole company runs seamlessly like a Swiss watch. Number two is clear measures and standards. There're clear measures for every single goal and every single person knows how they measure everything they're expected to accomplish. The third part is clear deadlines and schedules. Every single person knows what they have to do, when they have to do it, and how it's going to be measured. The final one that they found was surprising is big rewards for high performance, is the

20

most successful companies really pay their high performers well. At General Eclectic if a senior executive earns $500,000 a year and they hit their numbers and exceed their numbers, they can a million dollar bonus at the end of the year, so General Electric has what you'd call a performance culture. Everyone in that company is driven toward making sells, is to drive the numbers, and it's because the payoff can be substantial.

Anyway, that's what companies do, so that's what a leader does. If you want to develop a leader, they have to have very clear goals. Now, if you read the studies, why are top leaders from every type of company but including Fortune 500 companies, why are they fired, dehired, thrown out by their boards of directors? Because they didn't achieve the goals that were assigned to them and as a result people who've worked for decades to get the president of a Fortune 500 company are just thrown under the bus, because all the people care about in business today is results, goals and results. That's the most important thing.

If we're talking to people, and we're not talking to Fortune 500 CEOs here, those who are listening, if you're running your own business, ask yourself clearly "What is your number one goal for your business this year? Exactly how do you measure it and what is your schedule and who's responsible for achieving every part of it?" And people just go shaking their head, "But, but, but, but," they mutter. Most of the people listening to this are what are called solopreneurs, and solopreneurs are a huge multi-million person market today, and they're working by themselves, usually out of their own homes or small offices, and they're totally responsible for their financial results, and I have worked with rooms full of them and 80 or 90% of them are starving. They're taking the bus to travel. They've got holes in their shoes. Why? It's because they simply don't know this stuff, nobody ever told them. In order for you to be successful you have to have goals and measures and standards and deadlines and you have to sell all day long. The key to success in business is for the key people to be selling

80% of the time. What about paperwork and what about email? Check your email twice a day, check it at 11, check it at four. Turn it off and focus all of your time in face to face with customers, and if you'll do that, astonishingly enough your business will just explode.

Mike Agugliaro:	I love that. I love that. So Brian, you said there's 10 greats there, the leadership, the product, the business plan. What are some more of those 10 greats?
Brian Tracy:	Okay. The next great is a marketing plan, and a marketing plan is how you attract people to your offering. Now, often people are confused. What's the difference between marketing and sales? Well, the answer is marketing is attracting people by what is called the value proposition. The value proposition is the heart of the business. The value proposition is what your product or service does to change or improve the life of your customer, and the value proposition is not your product. For example, people say "Well, I sell insurance." That's not a value proposition. The value proposition is piece of mind and security for your family. That's what people want and need and will buy, and if they can get it with a Buddhist chant or a reading a book or taking a course or buying insurance, they don't care the process. Most people, and I spent seven years training business owners in my coaching programs, I say "Now, what I want you to do is I want to explain your company but do not tell us the name of your product, the name of your company, or your industry. Just explain your product in terms of how it changes the life a person who consumes it." It's astonishing, again that 80 20 rule, 80% or more of business owners cannot explain the value proposition of their product. In marketing what you have to do is you have to focus on the value proposition.

One of my favorite examples is when Steve Jobs came back into Apple and realized that Apple had a lot of problems and they needed a new product. They needed something to take them out of the dive that they were in, and they came up with the iPod. Now, the iPod was a remarkable development because it had three new business models. First of all, it contained music, enormous amount of music, electronically. Second of all, they negotiated contracts with all the major record companies to sell single songs for 99 cents. Third of all, they set up iTunes, a completely new electronic marketplace where people could go and buy instantly download music, and they put it all in your pocket with earbuds, and so they said "Now how are we going to sell this?" Because variations of these three propositions, three value propositions, had existed, and the answer they came up with was Apple iPod, 1,000 songs in your pocket, and they sold 50 million sets, and eventually became the most profitable company in the world.

Now that's the key. You should be able to explain your value proposition in less than 12 words, better five, but less than 12 words. If it takes more than that it means you don't even know what it is and all you're doing is your confusing prospects, so that's marketing. Marketing is to say "All right, what is our value proposition," and by the way this is a very complex subject. I spent hundreds of hours working on it, and then how do you summarize it in such a way that it bypasses the conscience mind and it connects with the emotions and it triggers the response "I want that. That's for me. I want that. I want that now." People, we find, in business make these decisions emotionally and justify logically. The value proposition has to connect the emotions like an electrical arc and cause the person to want it instantly without knowing anything about it just because of the way the value proposition is stated.

That's the marketing process and we teach that in detail, and we teach the seven parts of the marketing mix and the four pillars of marketing strategy and it's astonishing. If you are out of these, I call them the big eleven, the four pillars and the seven Ps, if you're missing any one of those your company will fail. That's it. It's like one blown tire when you're driving down the road in a brand new $100,000 car. One blown tire and the car is just a pile of metal until it's repaired. We teach all that.

Then we go on to having a great selling process. Now you have a marketing plan, so you're attracting people. People are raising their hands and saying "I want that. I want that." Now, you have to convince them to buy your product or service and pay you money for it, and it's astonishing. Again, going back to IBM, the biggest companies have found that the key to success in business is the ability to sell the product, and selling the product is a process. My Psychology of Selling program, which I put together many years ago, is the bestselling program in the history of man on Earth, outsold all other audio programs that have ever been produced on sales, because what it does is it systematically and logically explains the professional selling process, and it applies to everything from pencils to supercomputers, and I could tell you because I've spoken 31 times to IBM audiences on professional selling and other subjects, and also to people who sell pencils, and the principals are the same, and you know that 80 to 90% of business owners don't know them, and so when they meet a customer, they don't really know what to say and if it's anybody listening to this, hears the fatal words "Well, let me think about it."

"Let me think about it" is a way of saying "You are a lousy salesperson and you have not given me a single reason for buying your product" and "let me think about it" means "Goodbye forever. I never want to see you again." Sales people or business owners go out and they hear that all the time. Whenever I say that, cringe like you put a knife in their stomach. I cut my teeth on selling. I find that if you have a good product that's reasonably priced and you have a good market, you can go out and sell it. You can go out and sell it and you can make a living and you can make a great living.

Then if you want another great: is great people, and the process of hiring, managing, developing, training, supervising, motivating great people is massive, and most people don't even know how to hire. Most small business people, if they do get to the point of hiring, they hire their friends or they hire completely inappropriate

24

people or the hire the wrong, it's just the most amazing darn thing, and so we teach the entire process of hiring and motivating the best people and then we talk about great management. You're the leader, but how do you get great managers? And we go through the management development process and people just shake their head because these are all essential, absolutely essential elements to the success of a business, and most small and medium sized business owners, especially solopreneurs, have never heard them before. That's why the success rate of people who go through my program is just astonishing, and I give them a 200 page manual with every single point written out in detail, and they fill in the blanks and they do exercise and they come up with an action plan. It's like a whole new lease on life. It literally saves people's financial lives.

They say ignorance of the law is no excuse. Ignorance of the principles of business as an excuse is the guarantee for bankruptcy. Someone once said, "If you build it, they will come." If you build it, they will come is the formula for company bankruptcy because how do you know that anyone wants it before you build it, anyway.

Mike Agugliaro: That's such valid points, Brian. You went from taking us from a plan to the marketing to the selling to great people and you built it into a framework that allows people just to look at what they have. I bet you hear all the time, Brian, like, "Man, if I just had this five years ago or ten years ago." It probably would have removed a lot of pain from people, right?

Brian Tracy: Yeah it probably would have saved your life, financially. The thing is: learn it now. I had one gentleman, I just remembered, he came to my sales seminar. He was 52 years old, a little bit overweight. He'd been selling for his whole life, since he was 20 years old. He came to the seminar, I explained to him this is how you sell professionally and he'd never heard it before. All he was taught was basically high pressure selling where you lean in to the customer and you use all kinds of tricks and things like that.

I said, "No, no. Professional selling means that you establish a high quality relationship based on trust with customers and you help them to improve their life and work with your product. That's all you focus on." He wrote to me one month later, and he went back in with this, he'd never heard of it before, and his sales went up 400%. 52 years old, he said he'd never made more money in his whole life, and he's never had more fun selling. Before selling was just a job. Each time somebody came into his company it was "All right, here we go again" and then "get ready for the pressure." Now when they come in he smiles, he welcomes them, he thanks them for coming in and asked them about their life and their work. He doesn't even make any attempt to sell, and finally they say "Well, can I buy your product. Can you tell me about your product. I'd like to buy it." He said "it's just amazing." He could not believe the difference, and so learning these critical skills is essential.

Mike Agugliaro: Yeah, I love that. Now, Brian, I hear people all the time saying "Well, I have no time to get things done. I have no time to read books." What insights do you have to help somebody who uses that excuse about time to help them improve it?

Brian Tracy: Well, the fact is there's always time enough. It's just a really trite old saying. There's always time to do the most important things. I'm an expert in time management. I say that very gratuitously because I'm the bestselling author on time management in the world, in 42 language, but I still study. I did about three hours worth of studying this week, last week, on time management looking at some of the most current research, and one of beautiful little one liners I came across is it's not that people don't have the time it's just they haven't made a particular activity a priority. The key issue is priorities. What's more important and what's less important? That's why people like Warren Buffet, they're top priority is to study, and Warren Buffet was asked "What is your secret to success if you have one?" He said "simple," he said "I say no to everything except those two or three things I can do that make all the difference." Jeff Bezos, the same. Bill Gates, all successful people, Steve Jobs said the same thing. All success people learned to say no to everything. Whereas unsuccessful people, they don't have any time because they say yes to everything. They check every single email. They check every piece of spam and they check their Facebook. You know the average university student checks their Facebook 18 times an hour.

Mike Agugliaro:	Wow.

Brian Tracy:	The average working employee checks their email between 95 and 145 times a day, and it stays on, so every time a piece of spam comes in it goes bing. They just did a study on this and they compared email today, that bell that rings, they compared it to the sound of a slot machine going off in a casino, and whenever it goes off it triggers this ring goes, shiny objects, it triggers the anticipation in listener's mind "What did I win? What did I win?" Just like a slot machine where the coins go jiggling and bangling down and they say as soon as it goes off it's like the slot machine and they instantly, no matter what they're doing, they completely forget what they're doing and they go "what did I win?" And they turn instantly to their email to see what they just one. They cannot resist the sound of the bell, and so how do you?

What I do, I'm talking to you now, and I just turn off my sound, and pay no attention to the computer for hours at a time, because if the computer's on as soon as it goes off you go bing like a dog. Your ears go up, "What did I win?" The rule today now is don't check your email in the morning. Leave it off until 11:00. In fact, I'll give everybody who's listening to this a very simple formula to double their income and eventually become rich and successful. Are you ready?

Mike	Yes.

Agugliaro:

Brian Tracy: It's very simple. It's the essence of my bestselling book worldwide, is plan your day in advance the night before. Write down everything you have to do and then choose your highest priority, the one task that is more important and valuable than any other. Then, the next morning when you start work sit down and start work on that task. Leave everything off, phone off, computer off, everything off. When you say that to people sometimes they go through the same reaction as a drug addict having to go cold turkey. They actually shake at the very idea of not being able to check their email. The very idea of it just causes them to tremble because they're addicted to the sound of the bell.

In fact, physiologist have said that whenever the ding goes off, a shot of dopamine goes through your brain. Dopamine is the same chemical in cocaine, and what it does is it give you a stimulus and sort of a happy response. It's like, again, like the slot machine, so every time it goes off this shot of dopamine goes through your brain. Now you'll know, if you know anything about alcoholics, they say "One drink is too many and then there's no limit to how many drinks you can drink." Alcoholics, if they take one drink, drink until they pass out. What happens in the morning is the first time you take a shot of dopamine, you immediately become addicted and you get onto a treadmill and all day long you check emails.

That's why people check emails 95 to 145 times a day or more because you see people walking down the street. They have laws by the way, have seen these laws? You cannot walk while texting. Of course they've got lots of laws, no driving while texting, but you cannot walk while texting because people were actually walking out into traffic and being hit by cars. They're walking into posts and smashing their faces and have to be taken to the hospital. They're walking into people and knocking them down, so in large cities like New York there's laws against texting while walking because people can't stop.

28

You see them walking down the street talking and
texting with their earphones on, walking, talking, texting.
They can't stop. They're like dopamine dope addicts and
this is why people don't have time. They've got lot's of
time. If you told a person, if you get this done by the end
of the day you get a $100,000 bonus, I could promise
you they'd turn off their email and they'd turn off their
phone and they'd work themselves silly. They wouldn't
even eat if the motivation was high enough, so basically
if it's a matter of motivation then it's a matter of choice.
If you're not getting these other things done you are
choosing not to do them. You're just choosing to do
things of lower value.

Mike Agugliaro: My fingers are going wild typing notes because you're
giving so many golden nuggets here, Brian, especially
that dopamine. I mean it's almost like the Pavlov dog
right, ring the bell and the dog starts salivating, that's
amazing. Brian, you wrote a book, one of your books
was *Change Your Thinking Change Your Life: How to Unlock
Your Full Potential for Success and Achievement*, and I think a
lot of people feel that they have this potential either
shackled or it's held down. What kind of insight could
you give them to unlock some of this achievement?

Brian Tracy: Well, the starting point, I just keep coming back to it, I
meet people all over the world, and it's become a joke
because I say it in my seminars. They came up to me and
they said "I was at your seminar a year ago, two years
ago, and you've changed my life. You made me rich." I
get emails all the time, people come up to me "You
changed my life. You made me rich. You change my life.
You made me rich." I said "Well, what was it about my
material that brought about this result?" They smile, they
beam, and say "It was the goals. It was always the goals,
because before I heard you talk I didn't realize how
important goals were. I thought that if you had them in
your mind that was fine", but a goal that is not in writing
with clear, specific measures, standards, and deadlines is
merely a wish, it's fantasy. I say "it's like cigarette smoke
in a large room." It has no substance. It has no effect on
you at all.

The studies show that a person who has clear written goals and who works toward them every single day accomplishes and earns ten times as much as people who don't. In fact, they did a study, I read these all the time, millionaires and billionaires, they find that rich people 85% of rich people have one big goal that they work on every single day. Only 3% of poor people have one goal and they don't work on it that often. Rich people have goals and they work on them every day. My favorite word is always clarity, clarity, clarity. You've got to be absolutely clear about exactly what it is you want and then write it down and then set a deadline and then make a plan to achieve it and organize the plan into a checklist and then work your checklist every day the same as any builder, any mechanic, any designer, any contractor always works with a blue print, is you have to work from a blueprint for your life as well, and you start to accomplish five and ten times as much as people without the blueprint because with the blueprint you're just basically distracted by anything that happens.

I have a program which I call The Attraction of Distraction, and I go through this whole thing and talk about how we are living lives where we are hyper-distracted virtually all the time. We simply cannot stay on task, and it's getting worse and worse and worse because of electronic interruptions. Here's another thing that USA Today found is that if you are constantly responding to electronic interruptions, you can never get any work done because it takes about 17 minutes after you responded to ding, a bing, a beep, a ring, or something else for you to refocus on the task, and all the success in life comes from important task completion, completing important tasks.

If you complete important tasks you'll be successful, and if you can't you won't, and so what happens with people is they're constantly distracted. They never get their important tasks finished. At the end of the day they're stressed out, and here's what USA Today found is that you lose about one IQ point per hour. From the time you check your first email, you start to lose one IQ per hour, so by the end of the day you've lost about ten to twelve IQ points, and they could basically become stupider as the day goes on. By the end of the day, you're a little bit... you know... "what?"-faced. I asked this example of my audiences: "How many times have you the day where you've been checking your email all day long and you finally go home and honey says what would you like for dinner, and you can't even think. You cannot decide. Your mind is exhausted. You're burned out. 'Anything, I'll eat anything, just anything,' because you're so tired, your brain is so depleted you can't even decide what to eat." Everybody in the audience agrees because everybody has this experience. Unfortunately, some people have it every single day.

Mike Agugliaro:

Wow. Yeah, that's a really great point. Brian, what do you think are some things that business owners, if you had a crystal ball, we should be thinking about paying attention to in the future over the next three to five years?

Brian Tracy:

Well, the most important thing is to stay current, stay current. I read two or three books a week, plus I read a whole series of magazines, articles, and newsletters. I subscribe to Harvard Business Review, and I get reports from Harvard every single day online as part of my subscription. Plus, I have other online material that I get and then that leads to online material, so I keep current with the research findings. People say "Where do you get all these ideas?" I keep current with them. I spend time every single day reading these critical ideas, reading the magazines, underlining, writing in them, and so on. That's one of the things is keep current.

My friend Jim Rohn tells a story about it: he called into a company that was in serious trouble as a consultant, and the owner said "Please help me because my business is really struggling in what is a pretty good market for other people." He said "Sure." He said "but in order for me to help you, please give me the names of the best magazines and books that have been written in this industry in the last couple of years." The business owner "I have no idea." He said "I don't have time for that crap. I'm trying to make a living here." Jim says, he said "Well, I could have saved you a lot of time and money in consulting fees." He said "The reason you're going broke is you have no idea what's going on in your industry. How many industry conferences do you go to each year?" He doesn't go to any. You know the highest paid people in every industry or specialization go to all the conferences and they go all to the session and then they listen to all the people and then they network and ask questions and they pick up books and ideas and pamphlets and so on. The worst, the people who're starving, have always got a reason never to go near a learning experience. 80% of Americans have not read a book in five years.

Mike Agugliaro:	Wow.
Brian Tracy:	Most people never read a book, I've seen people 45 years old, never read a book after they left college. They just never read another book. Here's another thing. You learn about homes of rich people what do you see? You see bookcases and bookcases and piles and piles, far more books than you'll ever have a chance to read. We just collect books. There's a psychological principle behind it by the way, more research, is we buy books so that we have it handy just in case we need it, so your house, my house, wealthy people's houses are loaded with book that they've bought. They heard about it, somebody said it's a good idea, they flip through Amazon, bing bing, it's there the next day and they mean to read it. They haven't read it yet. Can you relate to this, yourself?
Mike Agugliaro:	Me, yeah. I mean I used to just walk in, if my wife, if we drove by a Barnes and Noble or something I think I would get like a twitch like "Hey, do you want to just go in there?" I don't think I've ever walked in a bookstore, Brian, without coming out with a book, and Amazon forget about it. I looking just in my area I'm sitting now, and I have like three or four books just here that I've bought that, you're right, it's just like when I'm ready I'm going to read them, so yeah I can relate 100% to.

Hey Brian, I want to get to a definite subject, because you hit something before that I think is something I hear all the time, it's about hiring and recruiting, and I constantly hear stuff like "there's no good people" or "it's hard to do", so can you shed a little bit of your wise wisdom on hiring and recruiting?

Brian Tracy: Well here's, they always say "Well, hire people who are better than you" but that's very hard to do unless you have a large company and lots of department. Generally speaking, you can only hire up to your own level. If you're undeveloped or if you're a new entrepreneur or if you're an experienced business person, that's the kind of people that you will hire. My friend Lloyd Conant, the founder of Nightingale Conant Corporation, once said that a ten never goes to work for a ten. If you're a ten the best you can hire is probably a five or a six. If you're a five or a six the best you can hire is a two or a three. Now, if you want to hire better people, you must become a better person yourself.

My friend John Maxwell calls it the law of the lid. He said "the experience, skill, and development of the leader is the lid on the business." If you want to raise the business and the caliber of the people in the business, you've got to raise the skill level and experience and knowledge of the leader. The leader is the lid who holds the business down or raises it up, so that's why it's astonishing if you as a business own just start to devote a certain amount of time each day to learning more about your business, learning more about marketing and selling. By the way, marketing and selling is the heartbeat, the "lub dub" of the business. Focus on that. The only way you can get better at marketing and selling is by doing it and doing more of it and doing it all the time and doing only that until you have so much money that you need to go to the Bahamas and count it, and it's not going to happen any time soon, but just focus on marketing and selling and marketing and selling and marketing and selling and making customers happy. If you'll do that then you'll be successful, and then you'll start to hire better people. You'll recognized better people because you cannot recognize someone that's really different from your own personally level.

Mike Agugliaro: Yeah, so it all starts with improving yourself first, because if you don't improve yourself then yeah I think the part you said, Brian, that really hit home for me is you could only hire up to your own level and then that quote "the leader is the lid that holds the business down or lifts it up." That's so resonating to me over a whole bunch of experiences that I can relate to on this. So Brian we have about five minutes left, and I'd like you to talk about anything that you feel is current going on with business owners. You're reading, you're out there, you're hearing. What are some things that you think people should maybe know about either habits or discipline or negotiations? Whatever you kind of want to serve of the next five minutes would be awesome.

Brian Tracy: By the way, I almost finished what I was saying and it has to do with your question, is successful people have what they call rituals. When I saw this the other day, successful people have rituals, and then I've seen it several times actually and I thought "Well, I wonder what that means?" And I simply realized that I have rituals and that successful people get up in the morning. The most common rituals by the way are rich people get up before 6 am. Poor people get up at the last minute possible, drink coffee, watch TV, wolf down a poor breakfast, and then race of to work, or they get, their working at home and they immediately turn on their computers and check their spam, but wealthy people get up at 6:00 and the first thing they do, most of them, is exercise. They exercise for 30 to 60 minutes. They really work they're body out because if you exercise in the morning, especially aerobic exercise, it pumps blood to your brain, pumps clear oxygenated blood to your brain, which actually increases your intelligence and creativity and keeps you sharp all day long. Most amazing thing, I learned that years ago.

Then the next thing that they do is they get ready for the day, get dressed, showered, shaved, get ready for the day,

34

and then they plan their day thoroughly in advance and get to work. I was saying earlier, if you want to be successful and had this very specific formula, get up, do your exercises, get prepared for the day, get dressed properly. Here's another thing by the way, people don't realize that the way you dress is the way you think about yourself. If you dress poorly, you think poorly about yourself. This has been proven in self imagine psychology for 80, is that your self-image, the way you see yourself, determines how you behave, how you think about yourself, your self-esteem, your self-confidence, your self-respect, so if people get up unshaven and dress like bums that just fell off a truck, well that's pretty much how they think about themselves.

In fact, I just went through this with someone. 95% of the first impression you make on other people is visual because before you say a word they just take a look at you, take a photograph of you in their minds, drop the photograph into their sub-conscience mind, the photograph is processed at about 8,000 time the speed of the conscience mind and they instantly get an intuitive feel of good, bad, smart, dumb, trustworthy, untrustworthy, good product. If you look like a bum your products are obviously of poor quality and over-priced, be careful. The ice is breaking under your feet dealing with this person, and nobody tells people this. I studied this exhaustively because I work at very high level with multi- multi-billion dollars corporations. One of my clients has 22,000 branches and 152,000 employees, and I work at the presidential level, and I could tell you when I go into a meeting with them I'm not wearing flip flops and a tee shirt and a tractor cap turned backwards.

The point is, if you get up in the morning, do your rituals, and then when you take start your work, start on your most important task and work on it nonstop for 90 minutes. Don't do anything. At the end of the 90 minutes, give yourself a reward, a coffee or walk around and stretch, come back again and then work for another 90 minutes nonstop. That'll get you to about 11 am.

Then as reward you can check your email, and the rule, again I've told you, but study on this subject, is called the 3 21 rule is you can check your email three times a day for 21 minutes max, so you get on it, you clear all up, and turn if off and be on and off in 21 minutes. 11:00, after you've done three solid hours of hard, important work, then you can give yourself a little treat and check your email and get your dopamine rush and so on and then turn it off again. If you'll do that every single day, get up in the morning, exercise, get started, work on your most important task for three hours, and then check your email, your income will go up three, four, five times in the next year, and if you don't it won't.

Mike Agugliaro:	I love that. Brian, give us a little bit of your thinking of if I say "Brian, what is wealth or the quickest way you believe people can get to wealth?" What would you tell them?
Brian Tracy:	Well, the average self-made millionaire in the United States based on decades of research takes 22 years from the time they decide to become a millionaire until the time they hit the number, average is 22 years. Too many people today have this fantasy idea that they could be a Mark Zuckerburg. I'll run into people and I say "What do you do?" They say "Well, I'm working on an email or an app, and it's going to make me rich." There's almost 1.5 million apps out there, 99% of them aren't working. 80 to 90% of the apps you download you never use. There's only a few that make money, and people are walking around saying "Well, I'm going to develop an app" or "I'm going to invest or give some money to my weird friend and he's going to develop an app and then we'll all be reach." It takes an average of 22 years of hard work and saving your money and putting your money carefully away and nurturing it like you would nurture a plant, a lily from the tropics, and people think well they could just do it quick. No. No. You're going to have to take a long time. Now, if you want to earn more money faster, sell more stuff.

I have a little thing that I do in my seminars, I say that "Why do you get up in the morning?" I ask people "Why do you get up in the morning" and they mumble or mutter and so on. I say "You get up in the morning, you go to work to make more money. Would you agree with that? Not earn less money or the same amount of money. You want to earn more money. Would everybody agree with that?" They say yes. Okay, so you get up in the morning for MMM, which is to make more money. Now how do you make more money in our society? Well, it's called SMS, and I say "SMS stands for sell more stuff." So MMM requires SMS. That's the only formula that you need. You could even say MMM=SMS, you know it'd be the little symbol that you use, so if you want to make more money faster, sell more stuff, and then keep the money. That's it. There's no other way, and if you think that there is well eventually you'll come around.

Mike Augugliaro:
Yeah, yeah and that is just really great. I just you know "wealth, sell more stuff" and I think people today need to pay attention. Brian, at this point, and I know most people listen to this, I mean you are a legend out there, but how would they find out more about you and what do you have going on that they might want to consider.

Brian Tracy:
Well, as I told you, I speak on a wide range of subjects. Just go briantracy.com and probably the best place to start is with our pre-goal setting guide that you can download or that you can fill out online and start with that. We offer a lot of free stuff so that people can get a sense, sort of like hors d'oeuvres, so people can get a sense for the quality of the material that we offer, and everything that we offer we unconditionally guarantee, so by all means go to briantracy.com and download our goal setting program and look at some of the other free things. Get onto our list and start to get our free emails and our contacts, and that's where you would start.

Mike Augugliaro:
That's great, Brian, and Brian I'm excited because you'll be coming out. Those that are listening to the, Brian will be at the November's Warrior Fast Track Academy, so I'm excited to have him give a lot of great information. Brian, I can't think you enough for being on this show

today. You delivered amazing value. Thank you.

Brian Tracy: Well, it's always a pleasure and wish you a great day as well. We could get to work. I've got to get back to making more stuff and selling more stuff. Thank you Mike.

Mike Agugliaro: That makes sense. You're very welcome, and everybody we don't leave this show without some gold nuggets. I'm going to go fast and furious. You gave us a lot of the ten greats right, great leadership, great product, great business plan, marketing plan, selling process, great people. What about this? Leaders are developed. Are you developing yours? The first job of a leader is to accept it, right, and achieve goals and have clear goals, have clear standards and measures. What about this? Clear deadlines and schedules, and guess what, the big performers, yeah they need to get big rewards and create a performance culture. Ask yourself clearly, what is your number one goal this year and who is responsible to achieve it? Key to success, he said, Brian said, is key people selling 80% of the time. Warren Buffets reads, and this was a good, this is something that success people, guess what, they're reading every day, right, and it's not time that's an issue, get this, it's a priority issue. I love that Brian said that.

How do you double your income? Plan your day in advance, choose your highest priority, and leave all the distractions off. Avoid those dopamine hits that Brian talked about. Create a clear blueprint and then what did he say? Guess what, you can only hire up to your own level, and he gave us oh and this one stuck out. I'm going to be talking to my business partner about this. The leader is the lip that holds business down or lifts it up. All managers need to understand that concept. Successful people have rituals. We're almost done here. There were some many golden nuggets. You're going to have to rewind and listen to this multiple times, and guess what. Wealth, sell more stuff, and he gave us the 3 21 rule, three times a day, check your email for 21 minutes. Well, that's it for this episode of the CEO

Warrior show. I'd be grateful if you could rate my show on iTunes. That helps me tremendously with keeping my show visible so that people that never heard it can discover it. If you've already done this, I'm very grateful. Be sure to connect with me on social media, great way to ask any questions. Until next time remember, massive wealth, tons of freedom, and market domination is only one action step away.

Key Lessons Learned:

Small Business

* Online networking is not working, small business needs to get out there and sell their product.
* Most people think they can sell a customized product the same way they can sell a transactional product.
* You need great leadership, someone with a clear vision and the responsibility for getting things done.
* You need a great product, 90% of success is due to having a great product. Increase the quality of your product first.
* You need a great business plan.
* The majority of small businesses don't have any of those.
* Ignorance of the laws of business results in bankruptcy.
* Keep current with what's happening in the world of business and your industry especially.

Leadership

* Leaders are developed, often self developed.
* Most large businesses spend a large amount of money training their leaders.
* Successful leaders learn constantly.
* If you emulate the great leaders, you can get similar results.
* The first job of a leader is to set business goals, you must have clarity. Clear goals and objectives, clear measures and standards, clear deadlines and schedules, and finally reward high performers well.
* Solopreneurs have to sell all day, every day.

Marketing Plans

- The value proposition is the heart of your business. It's not your product, it's the effect and emotion and how it can change the life of your customer.
- Marketing is not sales.
- Your value proposition should be explained in less than 12 words.
- Your marketing should connect with your customer's emotions.
- Marketing leads to selling, selling is a process. Focus on helping your potential customer and they will want to buy your product.

Time Management

- You have enough time, you just have to make it a priority.
- Say no to everything that doesn't make a big difference.
- The average person spends too much time on Facebook or email.
- Plan your day the night before, set your highest priority and then work on that in the morning, turn everything off until 11am.
- If the motivation is high enough, you will find the time.
- It takes about 17 minutes to get back on task if you allow yourself to be distracted.

Goals

- Goals that aren't written down are wishes.
- Rich people have goals that they work on nearly every day.
- Work with clarity, write your blueprint and work from it.

Hiring

- We can only hire people who are as good as we are.
- The best way to find better people is to improve the quality of the leader.
- You can't recognize someone that is above your own level.

Success

- Successful people have rituals. Successful people tend to get up early and exercise, then get ready for the day.

- How you dress is how you think about yourself. Don't look like a bum.
- Start on your most important task for 90 minutes, take a break, then do another 90 minutes.
- Check your email for no more than 21 minutes each day.
- It takes an average of 22 years to become a millionaire, from the moment you decide to become one. If you want to earn more money faster, sell more stuff.

Final Tips

- Leaders are developed, how about yours.
- Create a performance culture.
- Read every day.
- Plan your day in advance and work on your highest priority.
- Make more money by selling more stuff.

Learn more at BrianTracy.com

Take Action!

__ Stop doing actions (Actions you currently do now but should stop doing)

_____

_____

__ Keep doing actions (Actions you currently do now and should keep doing)

_____

_____

__ Start doing actions (Actions you don't do now but should start doing)

_____

_____

__ Who will do new actions? (Assign the action to yourself or someone else)

_____

_____

__ By when? (When will these actions be complete?)

_____

_____

CONVERSATION WITH CAMERON HEROLD

WHAT ENTREPRENEURS SHOULD BE THINKING ABOUT

CEOWARRIOR.com/podcast-cameron-herold/

In this episode of the CEO Warrior Podcast, Mike Augugliaro interviews Cameron Harold. Cameron is known around the world as the business growth guru. Cameron speaks from experience by guiding his clients to doubling their revenue in three years or less. He is a top rated speaker, author, and leader.

Main Questions Asked:
- What is going on in Cameron's world?
- What's the problem with meetings these days?
- Why do people highjack meetings?
- When is it time to have a meeting?
- What do you suggest when it comes to strategic thinking?
- What is the roadblock for entrepreneurs creating the vivid vision?

- Do you think people have fear around sharing a big future?
- Tell me about the second in command.
- What should entrepreneurs think about over the next few years?

Mike
Agugliaro:

Hello, everybody and welcome to the CEO Warrior Show. My name is Mike Agugliaro and this is a show dedicated to business owners, teaching you how to fast track your business growth and give you practical doable tips that you can implement today. Grab your pen and notepad and let's get started. Today, I will be interviewing Cameron Harold and we're going to talk about a whole bunch of stuff. I mean, we're going to talk about business vision and why meetings suck today, and how to hire maybe a second-in-command or maybe have someone help run your business.

Before I bring Cameron on, let me let you know a little bit about him. I mean, Cameron is known around the world as the business growth guru. I mean, he is the mastermind behind hundreds of companies' exponential growth. Cameron's built a dynamic consultancy. I mean, his current clients include a big four wireless carrier and a monarchy. I mean, what do his clients say they like most about him? He isn't a theory guy, right? They like that Cameron speaks only from experience. He's earned his reputation as the business growth guru by guiding his clients to double their profits and double their revenue in just three years or less.

I mean, Cameron was an entrepreneur from day one. I mean, at age 21, he had 14 employees. By 35, he'd helped build his first $200 million companies. By age of 42, Cameron engineered 1-800-GOT-JUNK's spectacular growth from $2 million to a $106 million in revenue, and 3,100 employees. He did that in just six years. I mean, his company has landed over 5,200 media placements in that same six years, including coverage on Oprah. Not only does Cameron know how to grow business, but his delivery from the stage is second to none. The current publisher of Forbes Magazine, Rich Karlgaard, stated Cameron Herold is the best speaker he ever heard, he hits grand slam. Guess what? It doesn't end when Cameron is off stage, he doesn't stop teaching.

He is the author of the global bestselling business book, Double Double. It's in its seventh printing and in multiple translations around the world. I mean, Cameron is a top-rated international speaker and he's been paid to speak in 26 countries. He's also a top-rated lecturer at EO/MIT's Entrepreneurial Masters Program, and a powerful and effective speaker at chief executive officer and chief operating officer leadership events around the world. It goes on and on. Without any further delay, Cameron, how are you today?

Cameron Herold: Good, Mike. How are you doing? Thanks for having me.

Mike Agugliaro: Yeah. I'm doing great. I got to tell you, I've done a lot of shows and podcasts here, Cameron, but I'm really excited to have you on today for a couple of reasons. One, I consider you a mentor of mine. Two, you've helped my own business. If it's okay with you, why don't we first start with, what's going on in Cameron's world right now?

Cameron Herold: Sure. I guess, I'm most excited about heading off for New York tomorrow with my 13-year-old son, taking him for his 13th birthday trip. I let all my kids pick a city to go to and tomorrow, Connor gets to go to New York. We're heading out for four days, taking him to a Yankees' game, going to go to a play. He's got his Pokémon Go ready to try to capture some Pokémon. We're going to tour New York City via Pokémon, so that's going to be kind of fun. In the … [crosstalk 00:04:21] world … Go ahead.

Mike Agugliaro: Yeah. No. I'm saying, that's so exciting. I love watching you be such an amazing father and helping people. It's just awesome. Keep going.

Cameron Herold:	Yeah. Thanks. No, I mean, at the end of the day, none of us are getting out of this alive. The only reason we do this is to serve ourselves and to create a better a better world for our families and ourselves. I'm really fortunate, I love doing what I do to make money, but I keep that in perspective. On the work side of things what I'm really excited about, I've got my new book Meetings Suck has just come out.
	I'm also launching the COO Alliance, which is the only network of its kind in the world for second-in-commands. There's so many groups for entrepreneurs to learn from, but there's never been a space for the COO to be able mastermind and learn together, so I'm super excited about that. Then I'm also coauthoring The Miracle Morning for Entrepreneurs with Hal Elrod and that's going to be in November. [Crosstalk 00:05:17] ...
Mike Agugliaro:	Wow. Yeah. That's exciting.
Cameron Herold:	Yeah. It's good stuff coming along ...
Mike Agugliaro:	Yeah. Let's dig in right into this. The first thing and I know that you've been talking about the subject for awhile, meetings suck. I mean, what's the problem with meetings in companies today?
Cameron Herold:	The reality is, meetings don't suck, we suck at running meetings. I was talking to a client of mine, a CEO that I coached about six, seven months ago and he was complaining about meetings. I said, have you ever trained any of your employees on how to run effective meetings? He said, no, I don't think so. I said, have you and your leadership team ever been trained on how to run effective meetings? He thought about it and he's like, no, I don't think so.
	I said, would we ever send our kid off to play little league baseball without teaching him how to hold a bat, throw a ball, and how to catch a ball? He's like, of course not. I'm like, we would send out kids to little league with more training than we would send our employees up to

go and run meetings or attend meetings or participate in meetings. I said, so maybe it's not the fact that meetings suck, maybe it's that we suck at running meetings. Really, that was the impetuous for the book was realizing that all we need to do is give people the basic skills and they can actually be quite successful.

Mike
Agugliaro:

Yeah. That's awesome. Can you share with us some of the maybe simple framework that somebody listening could just … maybe they can relate to what you've learned that people are doing wrong with meetings? Then maybe you can just share a little insight like, guys or gals, we got both listeners, here's some things you could think about just to change the game in your business and meetings.

Cameron
Herold:

Sure. I'll give you the kind of the core basics that's really easy for any company to put in place. Every meeting has to have a clear purpose. Just one sentence, why are we here? If you're booking a meeting and requesting people to attend something, in the meeting notes or in the subject line, you put down the purpose of the meeting, one sentence. Every meeting can have a maximum of three outcomes. Just what are the three big things that you're going to get done? Those also go into the meeting's notes so that people can accept or reject the meeting when they see why they're coming. Every meeting has to have a clear agenda. Just what are you covering, in what order are you covering it, and how many minutes are you going to spend on each agenda item?

Really, I allow people to say no agenda, no "attenda". At the end of the day, why do we have so many people coming to meetings when the reality is some people don't even really need to be there? We'd rather have them being back at their desk and applying their time and resources on something they're really into or we really need them to work on. That's the first part, purpose, outcomes, and agenda. The second part of this is, book every meeting for half the time you first think about booking it for. At the end of the day, if you're booking it for an hour, book it for 30 minutes. You're going to end up getting it done in less time, you'll control the idle chatter, you'll have a moderator or a timekeeper. Book it for half the time you first think about booking it for.

Every meeting should start exactly on time. There's really no reason why meetings should start late. In fact, I think the only reason that we do start late is because we book everything back-to-back. What I like doing is I like finishing every meeting five minutes prior to the schedule of the ending time. That allows you to have time to actually walk down the hall, talk to your assistants, get a glass of water, grab a coffee, check your email, and start your next phone call or your next meeting exactly on time.

Starting everything on time, stopping everything five minutes early, and then I also put a moderator and a timekeeper in a parking lot in place, so any good items that come up that you want to discuss that maybe aren't on the agenda can be written down and you can talk about those when the meeting is over or you can take it off-line. Those are really the core tenets of, I think, of highly effective meetings.

Mike Agugliaro:	Wow. That is like gold there. My fingers, I'm like typing away here. Cameron, would this apply … ? Here's what I'm thinking. Let's say we haven't been doing this structure, so what's my first step to get my team to understand this new structure? Should I just put this stuff in place like, purpose, outcome, and agenda? Or should I have a meeting to teach them on it? Run us through how to implement it now into our company.
Cameron Herold:	Yeah. I mean, and I'm not here trying to sell a book, but the easiest way to try to get this done is get every employee a copy of the book, Meetings Suck, and have them read it before they go to their next meeting. The reality is I've literally laid it out for them. I structured the book in a way that a third of the book is written for the people booking and running meetings. A third of the

book is written for the people that are attending and just participating in meetings.

Then the other third of the book talks about specific meetings that you need to have in your company and kind of how to setup those meeting rhythms. I've really set it up as a very easy to digest bible in a way to give you the structures for meetings. It was written in a nice short format, it's about 110 pages in total, so it's only a couple-hour read. The people can literally create their meeting rhythms for their company right out of this book.

Mike Agugliaro:	Yeah. I love that.
Cameron Herold:	If you want to go around that and you don't want to read the book, okay. Then, let me tell you what the basics are, don't allow anyone to attend the meeting unless the person booking it puts the purpose, outcome, and agenda right in the meeting notes. Allow people to say, no agenda, no attenda.
Mike Agugliaro:	Yeah. That's going to change things already. Because I know when I've run meetings, you come in there, you have your own personal agenda, then … Do you think this happens, Cameron, because there's no structure, all of a sudden they throw … like some are talking about one thing and someone … I've always been curious why they do this, someone all of a sudden say something from completely left field, has nothing to do about why we're there, and all of a sudden it twits everything out? Why do the people throw things from left field?
Cameron Herold:	There's a few reason for it. The first one is if you don't put an agenda in place, just what are we covering, in what order are we covering it, and how many minutes are we going to spend on each agenda item, people don't realize that the time is under constraint. You know, it's Parkinson's law that stuff expands to fill the space that we give it. If you don't give a small timeline, half the time you first think about booking it for, and you don't show people what we're covering and in what order, then they think they can have all these random discussions. The

parking lot also allows you, hey, that's a great point, but it not on the agenda. Let's write it down and we'll cover it, we're just not going to cover it right now.

You keep going back to the meeting, going back to the meeting, and people don't take it personally. The second reason that people tend to go off on these little hyperlinks is that there really is no system or control in place to get the quieter, analytical, amiable people to speak as well. I even outlined in the book Meetings Suck how to get the quieter people to be contributing using a Post-it note exercise that I learned from General Electric. Then the third reason is that you don't have a moderator. You don't have someone who is appointed in advance of the meeting starting to be able to say, hey, Bob, great thing, but let's stay on topic. You don't have that first role that everyone respects. When you do that, everything can be brought back in alignment quite quickly.

Mike Agugliaro:	Could I use this same structure, Cameron, if I'm say running my company remotely on doing maybe video or Skype conferencing? That's the one question. Could I use it remotely and two, could use this structure with them and have a meeting with one of my vendors? Could I just send them a pre-agenda and just put them in the structure without teaching the vendor?
Cameron Herold:	Yeah. In fact, that's what I suggest in the book Meetings Suck as well is that you start to actually follow these rules with your customers, with your suppliers, with your employees, and remote employees, and people start to fall in line. As an example, we started doing this podcast right at the top of the hour, which means by my rules, we'll be finishing five minutes prior to the end of the hour. We'll finish at the 55-minute mark. In that way, we can finish everything up on time and start the next thing exactly at the promised time.

When you do that with customers and suppliers, it blows them away because nobody respects their time. It not only shows that you guys have some discipline thought and discipline action in place, but you also respect them as much as you respect the time. People love that system. Regarding the remote employees, I have all of my meetings over at a product called Zoom. I switched off Skype about 18 months ago to Zoom. A really easy platform, very efficient, you can record calls, the digital quality is very, very high. It's not as kludgy as Skype has become. I also use other products like Stormboard and Google Docs, so we can actually be updating documents live on the fly as we're discussing, and just really easy to use tools for people across platforms.

Mike Agugliaro: I love that. Now, you've given me the structure that I need to be done here five minutes before ... [crosstalk 00:14:16]. It gives the framework. You just showed real-time how that applies. Okay. I know, Cameron, it's funny doing some of my own events, people, you talk to them and they're like, I got a meeting at 12 o'clock or one o'clock or two o'clock or five o'clock. Now, they have a structure. What would you tell people to think about when they should have a meeting? What should they be identifying maybe [running 00:14:41] in their company? I know this is a big broad stoke, but I want people to understand what they should even think when it's time to have the meeting to put in the structure.

Cameron Herold: Right. You don't actually create the structure second. What you do is you figure out the need for something and then you create a meeting rhythm around that. The examples would be, every company needs to have an annual retreat to plan out their goals and plan out their year. Usually, a one or a two-day off-site retreat held in September or October, two to three months prior to the start of your calendar year. Every company needs a quarterly retreat to get the leadership off site for half a day to a full day to press reset on that plan, review the Vivid Vision, come up with the goals for the quarter. That happens usually two to three weeks prior to the start of every quarter. Every company should have time in their calendar for strategic thinking.

Now, I don't like the term strategic planning because

those two words really don't fit well together. You can't have strategy and planning, they're very different. I have strategic thinking systems to talk about the future, what if stuff might happen, what if the good stuff happens, what if the bad stuff happens? Just to be brainstorming and throwing ideas around. I usually like to do two to three hours every month for just strategic thinking. I also like to have a one to two-hour finance meeting with the leadership team every month where we review the P&L in detail, we review the balance sheet in detail, and we teach people how the financial statements work and link together, so people start getting a deeper understanding of how a business really runs.

We all run the business together as a team using that finance meeting. We then have our weekly war meeting where the leadership gets together and looks at what our updates are, what each person is working on, we review the dashboards and KPIs together, and then we help unstick people if people if people on the leadership team are stuck. That's the weekly meeting that's held usually on a Monday for 60 to 90 minutes. Then you coach all of your individual direct reports for a one-hour or 30-minute coaching meeting depending on the depth of their role.

That's when you help direct them and give them the emotional support and also give them the systems or the growth if they need the skill set growth. That's really the core types of meetings. Then outside of that, the only one that I throw in is the daily huddle. It's something we learned from Verne Harnish in Rockefeller Habits. It's just an all company's seven minutes standup meeting that happens usually around 11 o'clock or two o'clock, and I kind of outlined that pretty good detail as well.

Mike Agugliaro:	Inside, Cameron, so everybody who's listening is clear, inside the book Meetings Suck, do you cover all the different meetings or should, is that something that's covered in Double Double?
Cameron	I cover it all in the book Meetings Suck, I also cover it in

Herold:	a little bit less detail in Double Double. Really, I took kind of the core content around meetings from Double Double and really expanded on it. You know, the book Double Double was written five years ago. In the last five years, I've coached probably 60 or 70 other high-growth companies and just learned a lot more about what starts to really make meetings work. Also, I answered a lot more of the questions that I probably had in my head and thought I'd written down for Double Double, but hadn't really included. There's a lot more depth in Meetings Suck with people … [crosstalk 00:18:05]
Mike Agugliaro:	Yeah. Listeners out there, just go buy both of them. Like Cameron said, he's not here to sell books. I haven't read the Meetings Suck book yet, but I already have it sitting here on Amazon for myself to order it for all my members in my company. The Double Double is an awesome book to just get it because this type of wisdom is of, you implement one thing and it could change the game. Cameron, before we move off the conversation about Meetings Suck, is there anything else that they should know about it? Then I want to move into business vision.
Cameron Herold:	Let me think, is there anything else that you need to know about meetings? One thing around meetings is that the CEO, the leader should really speak last. At the end of the day, the CEO's job is to grow people so that people can grow our companies for us. The CEO's job is not to always have the right answers, it's not to always be the one speaking and directing and leading people, it's to really grow them.
	What we want to do is ask the questions, ask the strategic and leadership questions, let the team start to figure stuff out. If we speak last, we're often going to hear that they have the same ideas that we might have had as well. By giving them the ability to speak first, it grows their confidence and their competence. I really, really encourage the most senior people in the room to speak last, and to get the most junior and newest people in the

room to speak first. It really starts to grow and develop your team, which is what leadership is all about.

Mike Agugliaro:

I love that. That just makes so much sense. Especially the part … I want to go back to the strategic thinking. For all of you that are listening, you'll see a common thread amongst the very successful people out there like Cameron and I've spent a couple of days just a month ago with Frank Kern at his home, and you'll see the strategic thinking, I don't want to run over that, you guys will find true power when you just set that time aside to just go through that. You know what, Cameron? That made think of a question. When people are sitting down, what is your format that you tell somebody when you're going to do strategic thinking? Here's a couple steps you should do, maybe be in a quiet place, what would you tell them to do?

Cameron Herold:

Sure. I like to get outside of the office, get away from the laptops, get away from the computers, and pull a whole stack of Post-it notes together. I use the system that General Electric gave us. By the way, my whole rule in business is that it's already been thought of. For the most part, some companies have spent millions of dollars figuring everything out, just do what the best do. If General Electric and Starbucks use the exact same system for strategic thinking, shit, I'm just going to use that. I'm going to use a simplified version.

What I do is I start thinking about the goals first, where am I taking my company, what's my revenue goal, what's my profit goal, what's my customer engagement goal, what's my employee engagement goal, and what's my strategic thrust for the year? Those five goals point me in the direction of my Vivid Vision. I put the numerical goals in place for each of those five first. Then I'd start thinking about what are all the projects I could do, what are all the things I could put in place that will make those goals happen? If I nail these seven or 70 projects, the goals would happen for sure.

I throw all the projects up on the wall, and then I vote

54

on the projects as to which ones are the easiest to put in place quickly and which ones are going to have the highest impact. I try to put in place as many of the projects that are easy to put in place, that are not complex, that are not costly, because I recognize that momentum creates momentum. That's kind of how I work it. Then I usually try to eliminate as many projects as I can, because you're always going to have a million great ideas, but the key is not to execute on all the great ideas and say no to all the hairy ones, all the complex ones, and to put the things in place that will create momentum for you.

Mike Agugliaro: Yeah. That's really awesome. Based on that and that seems like it's going to be a great lead into talking about vision. What would you give if I said, what should people think about the word delegation or the act of delegating? What would you tell the listeners to think about?

Cameron Herold: I guess two parts. You need to delegate at certain times and specific ways for specific things, but you don't start with delegation. You start with inspiration and kind of information. You really want to lead people by showing them where you're going by explaining what your outputs are and what your future looks like, so they can start figuring out how to make it happen. The best analogy I could come up with here would be someone who's building their dream home. You know, I would have an idea of what I want the dream home to look like.

I would pull drawings and photos out of magazines and sketches then I would take pictures of friends' houses and I'd pull all this stuff together and I'd share it with the contractor and I'd say, build me a house that looks and feels like this. Then the contractor would go away with my visions and they would create the plans, the blueprints to make my visions come true. Then they would hand the plans to the workers and the workers would recreate it. In that sense, I haven't delegated anything. I've just given clarity around my vision and I've shown them where I'm going.

Now, the contractor will probably delegate some parts of that out. He'll say to the electrician, you do the electrical, and the plumber, you do the plumbing. He's not telling them how to do the work, he's just telling them what the finish looks like. You know, here's what the schematics or the electrical need to look like, here's roughly where I want plugs to be in the room, but he's not going to tell them how to do the wiring. I think, too often, we tell people how to do stuff instead of very clearly telling them what we want built.

Mike
Agugliaro:

Yeah. That's really awesome. That puts around ... so take us now that we talked about clarity. You've mentioned vision a couple of times now, take us into whole subject of the power of creating your philosophy on visions.

Cameron
Herold:

Sure. I think we've all experienced the traditional classroom type, the NBA type of mission statement or vision statement. Get all your employees into a room, put all your favorite words up on a whiteboard, let's vote on our favorite words and come up with a six or seven words that most inspire us, then let's match all those words up into a sentence and that's supposed to be our mission statement. You know, go team. The reality is nobody is aligned with that. Nobody really understands what it all means. Even the entrepreneur usually walks in the meeting saying, that's kind of [inaudible 00:24:50]. It really is not. I have a better picture in my head of what the company looks like. They're not what [someone 00:24:55] says.

The idea of the Vivid Vision is very different. The Vivid Vision is the entrepreneur leaning out into the future and describing every aspect of their company as if it's been completely [built out 00:25:09]. You describe your company three years from today, December 31st, three years from now in its finished state. You describe what the customers are saying about your company. You describe what the employees are saying. You write down what the media is writing about you. You describe operations and IT and finance, marketing. You really describe the every single business area of the company, and you describe it as if you're standing in your company, looking around describing what you see and what you feel.

Now, if you've gone into the future three years from now, you don't know how it happened but you know what it looks like. That's the key is to explain what it looks and feels like versus how you made it happened. Very much like the homeowner who explains what the finished house looks like, the team will figure out how to build the house, but it's your job to explain what the finished state looks like. The Vivid Visions becomes the three or four page written document that describes your company inasmuch detail as possible so the team can figure out how to make it happen.

Mike Agugliaro:	What happens if somebody is … because I see that a lot with people, what if they're stuck, what if they just really struggle to see their future? Because I hear a lot of people that come to my events, Cameron, they're like, I want to grow to three million, whatever it is. In the way you laid it out, that's not enough clarity just to say three million. Correct?
Cameron Herold:	Correct. Three million is simply a goal. What I'm looking for is less than a goal and more about describing the company in its finished state. Describing the meeting rhythms, describing your culture, describing how everything fits together, actually give out samples of Vivid Visions from different companies. If any of you listeners want to download some, I can send you a link and they can download three or four specific examples to maybe get some clarity. A goal is very different from a full vision. If I was describing … Again, four pages of written description is much more than $3 million in revenue.

You know, $3 million in revenue doesn't describe how people are feeling, and how the leadership team looks, and what your recruiting efforts are like, and what your office environment looks and feels like. It's like saying, I want to have a craftsman style home, period, or here's pictures of how the living room looks, and here's pictures of the dining room looks, and here's the kitchen. It's just way more descriptive than simply one sentence. I think what happens is people have never encountered this idea of a Vivid Vision before, so they've had it in their mind, but they no one's ever helped them take it out of their mind and put it in paper.

If you ask the average entrepreneur to describe what their company looks like in the future and you spend 20 minutes asking them some questions, you'll be amazed at what comes out of their mind. I also like everyone when they're writing their Vivid Vision, I used to call it a painted picture, but I like them to get out of their office and go sit somewhere where they're inspired, somewhere around nature. Go get out of the office, no laptop, no ThinkPad, and take a notepad and a pen and just start mind mapping of the different areas of the business, and so you got a lot of ideas scribbled down. Then you can start to pull it altogether and figure out how to make it happen later.

Mike Agugliaro: Yeah. That's awesome, especially the mind mapping part. I remember when we did ours, which is years and years ago when we worked with you. I think it was me and my business partner, Rob, we had a lot of conversations around ... At that point, we found out, maybe this is helpful for some listeners. We like recorded our conversation that we were having back and forth, we had that transcribed and we sent to a ... I guess, it was copywriter/writer, who just kind of pulled it apart and said, look, does this look right? What do you think is the biggest roadblock, Cameron, with people? Because I've seen you talk about this at EO, I've seen you talked about this for years and years, but it still seems like a lot of people don't do it. What's the roadblock for people why they don't get this done?

Cameron Herold: I think the roadblock is entrepreneurs are pretty stubborn and they're never going to do as they're told. What they do is they sit at their desk in their boardroom with their laptop and they try to write their Vivid Vision and they can't figure it out. That's number one. Get the fuck out of your office, go somewhere around nature, around the lake, around the river, with trees, take your shoes off, sit on the grass with a notepad for four hours, put your headphones on, listen to The Grateful Dead, and just let your minds rest and daydream about the future. The second thing is that entrepreneurs love to dig in and figure out how to make it happen, so they often spend more time thinking about the plan than describing the future.

They end up pulling more of the plan as to how they're going to make it happen instead of describing what it looks like. Too often, people are trying to take what we have and make it bigger. Kind of taking the ball of elastic bands and keep adding elastic bands to it until the ball is bigger, instead of saying, what I actually want to build is a restaurant chain instead of a big ball of elastic bands. Allow yourself just to drift off, lean in into the future, describe what you're building, and then you'll see how much bigger it all of a sudden becomes. It's interesting, because I'm actually working on my 2019 Vivid Vision right now because my 2016 is wrapping up, and I'm realizing that my business three years from now looks completely different from what my business looks like today.

Mostly because I have five other books that have come out and I have the launch of the COO Alliance, which is really gaining quick traction, and my coaching model has really hit a pretty solid mark where my fees are getting to be very substantial. My business just looks and feels very different from what it did when I wrote my 2016 Vivid Vision three years ago. I'm creating that creative tension, I don't know how the heck I'm going to make it happen, but I really do know what it starts to look and feel like when I daydream and think about the future.

Mike Agugliaro:	Tell us about that word you just said, creative tension. It's the tension, the part where you're figuring it out and you have to push yourself to get it. Explain that so I have

more clarity around that.

Cameron Herold:
Yeah. The creative tension is that I know that this is what it looks like, but I haven't got a clue how to make it happen yet. It's kind of the homeowner who says, this is what I like to build but I don't know how to do construction, I don't know how to do electrical. They don't stop on their idea of building your dream home, they go and find the great contractor who has built similar dream homes who can build theirs. For your business, it's the same thing. When you're very clear on what you're building and you start sharing your Vivid Vision with people, people conspire to help make it happen for you. As an example, I'm in Joe Polish's 25K, his Genius Network Event, and literally ripping off everything from that event R&D-ing it to make the COO Alliance.

Joe knows that. Joe and I set our daily goals together and Joe is helping me at every turn to literally craft a very similar model to the Genius Network, but make it for second-in-commands only. When you tell people what you're building, they help you figure it out. I was just at the conference last week called Camp Maverick talking constantly about the COO Alliance, I had a couple of people interview me while I was there for their podcast, I had two people sign up their COOs for it, and I had one offer to do LinkedIn marketing for me. When you don't tell people what you're building, when you don't tell people what your future looks like, they assume that all you're working on is making today just a little bit bigger.

Mike Agugliaro:
That's great. I love the word creative tension. I'm going to use that, because when I first started getting into this coaching world and helping other people, I had a totally different name. When I was trying to find a word. I remember going to the beach with my wife and it's kind of like Buddha sitting by the tree, like, he refuses to leave even if he dies until he hits enlightenment. That's when I created this CEO Warrior. Now you've given me a real understanding of that creative tension. That's awesome. Thank you for that gift there.

Cameron Herold:	I remember when you were starting off in this coaching world three or four years ago, you didn't really know how it was going to happen. You just had this dawning that you knew you could add value, you knew you had a tribe that wasn't being addressed, you knew that you'd figure it out as you went, and you were just like, screw it, I'm just going it, and you just kind of dove in. I know for sure that whatever you're doing today in your sessions, it's probably very different from the first one you ever ran. It just keeps getting stronger and better, but you knew in your mind what it looked and you also trusted you'd figure it out as you go.
Mike Agugliaro:	Yeah. Do you think, Cameron, people have ... they have fear around sharing a big future. The reason I say this, I mean, for myself personally, I guess, I've got outgrown maybe some of my friends and there became a point where especially, like you said, this free the entrepreneur world family, I'm not quite sure they relate with me 100%. I find myself doing this. Like, I wouldn't share my big future because I was afraid like they're not doing good. Is that a common thing you see today?
Cameron Herold:	Yeah. I think people are afraid to share their future for a few reasons. One, we often surround ourselves with people that we've grown up with and that group doesn't think the way that we're now thinking. It's like when you hear about a couple or a husband and wife and they've just grown in different directions or grown apart. I think it often happens with our friends as well that the more successful you become, the more you start spending time around more successful people and you might drift away from people who are in just day-to-day jobs with day-to-day lives. That's okay, but it doesn't necessarily feed you, so sometimes you feel bad about sharing your big goals and big dreams with them. That might be one. The second one, I think, is we're definitely afraid of being judged.

We're so used too often, entrepreneurs didn't do well in school. We struggled in school, we're often the C students. We don't want to fail, we don't want to be that we're doing poorly, so we're afraid of sharing our big goals with people. I think we have a little bit of that built-in insecurity there. I think when we realize that the more you share your dreams and your visions with people, they're going to conspire to help you make it happen, they're going to line up behind you. I think it's just easier to share where you're going and trust the people are going to have your best interest at heart.

Mike Agugliaro: Yeah. I agree with you on that. What would you tell people, Cameron, about … one thing that I'm a big believer in and I'm wondering how you feel about it. I mean, I've spent wow, over $800,000, I'm making sure I learned from the greatest on the planet, from being in Genius Network and hanging out with Jay Abraham and Frank Kern. I mean, the list goes on, Disney and Zappos and yourself, being mentored by you. What insight would you give people about thinking about getting around or reading or anything about getting around really smart people who have done it?

Cameron Herold: Sure. A few points … I mean, I had a saying for the last couple of years that you network is your net worth. You know, the data point is actually there that the money that you earn today or your income is the average of the five people you spend the most time with. If you consider that for a second that whoever you're spending time with is actually impacting how much money you make. It's also the same with your fitness level, your physical fitness level is the average of the five people you spend the most time with. You want to start spending time with successful people, driven people, focused people.

Like you mentioned, Genius Network, Jay Abraham. I was on a call with Jay Abraham, four, five, six days ago I did a call with Jay Abraham. I'm in Dan Sullivan's 10x Strategic Coach Program, I'm part of the Masterminds Talks group, I've gone four years in a row. I'm part of the Maverick Group with Camp Maverick. I'm often surrounding my … and I also go to probably 25 events a year with YPO and with EO. I'm always surrounding myself with these better business people. The key though is to not show up and just learn at random. I think, too often, people are learning but they're not really putting it in place. What I like to do is summarize what I learned from those events, and then commit to putting some things in action.

As an example, on my top three today, one of my top three things I need to get done is I'm writing up all of my notes from Camp Maverick last week and committing to the top 10 action items from the event that I went to. I also use an app called CommitTo3, it's a free app, and I commit my daily top three business goals to Joe Polish and he'll commit his daily top three goals to me. On a daily basis, I have an accountability partner.

I think that's where a lot of people become seminar and learning junkies, but they don't necessarily put the ideas in place. I would really encourage people to almost act as if they're reporting to someone else. If you had to report to someone and say, I was out of the office for four days at this conference, I spent $5,000, cost of travel being there, here is what the business is going to benefit from, here is what I'm putting in place, people would be much better off.

Mike Agugliaro:	Yeah. I love that. I make sure I tell my team when we go to different conferences and stuff like, look, we go for one reason, we need to find a million dollars there. Otherwise, it's a complete waste, which sets their framework to look. I also love what you're talking about, just going to these things and not implement. I always say like expansion, personal expansion without execution is a total waste of time and energy. Okay. Cool. I want to make sure we have time to get to something and I think we have like 12 minutes before we finish our … [crosstalk 00:39:17]. You got me functioning in your meeting [crosstalk 00:39:21], so I'm excited about that. Let's talk about this whole second-in-command helping run a business, walk me through this whole concept.
Cameron Herold:	Sure. At some point, everyone's business starts to scale or you're definitely going to flatline, which is fine. You

can keep you business the same size forever, but at some point, you're probably going to want to grow and scale your business. Often, people look to bring on a second-in-command, a chief operating officer or a VP of operations or a general manager to help them run the company. What I always get nervous of is the people that do that too soon. If you don't have an assistant, you are one. What I really want people to consider is how do you actually bring on an executive assistant before you bring on that true second-in-command?

First off to start with that. When you know for sure that you are ready to bring the COO as a second-in-command, what I want you to do is write down the top five things that you need that person to get done in the first 12 months that they're with you. What are the big core projects that you need this COO to get accomplished? If they got them done, you'd have been thrilled at your decision to hire them. Then also think about the behavioral traits you want them to live by. How do you want them to fit together with you? Because at the end of the day, the COO is really your yin and yang. Right?

It's really that almost like the husband and wife growing a family together. It needs to be your better half. It needs to be that additional part of you that is going to help you scale. Really, making a list of what you need them to get, and then also what do you need them to or how do you need them to act. Then also look at what's on your list that you love to do that you would do for free, except your kids like to eat, and make sure you keep that stuff on your plate. Delegate everything except genius. You don't want to hire someone who has the same core strengths as you. You want someone who can have complementary strengths to you.

Mike Agugliaro:
Man, that was great framework for people to think about. Do you see, Cameron, ever that maybe there's a problem of ... is there a fear of letting go of responsibility?

Cameron Herold:	Yeah. I think there's often a fear of that. I think we often maybe don't even have that cognizant fear. I think we're often these radically self-reliant people who were stubborn. That's why we started our company, we didn't want to work for somebody else or we saw better ways, so we are narcissistic and that's to think that we can do it better. What we end up doing is building the habits of doing it ourselves, doing it ourselves, doing it ourselves, instead of hiring people to do it for us. I think in some way, we may have almost been misinformed by our grandparents. Our grandparents gave us that Protestant work ethic of work hard, work hard. I remember my grandfather, he's an entrepreneur, but every time I left his house, he would say, keep your nose to the grindstone.

I wish he would have said, work smart, be a little lazy, outsource more, hire people to do it for you. Instead, what he was telling me to do is to work hard, and I think entrepreneurs often work hard instead of working smart. Imagine if you took a list of everything that was on your plate that you did for over a course of a month, and imagine if you videoed yourself for a whole month and wrote down everything that you did, checked emails, replied to emails, attended meetings, spoke to meetings, proofread documents, whatever, and you just kept making a list of all these things that you did day to day in your company.

Then you categorized all of those things that you do in one to four ways, either I for incompetent, C for competent, E for excellent, or U for unique ability. Incompetent is you suck at it, you're just not really good at it. The competent is you're okay at it. Excellent is you're really, really good at it, but you don't love doing it. Then the unique ability is the stuff that you're really, really good at and you would do it for free, except your kids like to eat. Imagine if you could start delegating or outsourcing everything that you're incompetent, competent, and finally even excellent, so that the only things you're left doing are the stuff that you get energized from.

For me, I get energized doing speaking events, I get energized coaching, I get energized growing entrepreneurs, I get energized doing podcasts. Anything else, I'm pretty much drained at, it's just a lot of work. If you can get everything off your plate so that all you do is the stuff that gives you energy, business is going to grow like crazy, and then you're also surrounding yourself with people who love doing those other things as well.

Mike Agugliaro:

That's awesome. What should we think, Cameron, about creating a ... I'd love to hear your feedback. There's a lot of buzz out there, create a lifestyle business and ... What are your thoughts to ... wise words to give people about creating a business that serves them, instead of serves maybe against some business owners?

Cameron Herold:

A lifestyle business has gotten an almost a new definition. Lifestyle business nowadays tends to mean someone who travels around and doesn't have to go into an office, that has a business that throws off cash. You could have that exact same business with 500 employees. I mean, that's what my grandfather's company did, that's what my dad's company did. My dad was taking every Saturday, every weekend, every night off, he was taking every Wednesday afternoon off, he took tons of vacations because he built a business that ran without him.

Now, a lifestyle business ... that's why we start businesses is to give ourselves the cash to do what we want, to give ourselves the free time, but we end up often losing sight of that and we make the business our reason for waking up in the morning. That's mostly because we've become boring, it's not because our business needs us. It's because we've lost track of our hobbies and our joys and our excitement.

Remember when you got started this podcast with me and you asked me what I'm most excited about, I said, my trip to New York tomorrow. Like, I'm really excited about going to New York City for four days and I'll tell you what. All day, Thursday, Friday, Saturday, Sunday,

I'm not checking emails, I'm not checking phone calls, I'm not doing any work, because I want to hang out. If that's a lifestyle business, then awesome, because that's what my business is supposed to be. It's why I don't want to go to work every day and get three weeks holidays.

Mike Agugliaro:
Yeah. That's really great. It's great for people to think about that, too. If you were to tell … let's put you on a stage, but this stage has a million entrepreneurs, they all want to go to the next level and you were to go on just a one-minute rant or less and tell them, here's what you really should really think about, everybody, in the future, in your life, just considerations to maybe think about, what would you tell them?

Cameron Herold:
One thing is, where do you want to end up? Stephen Covey talked about begin with the end in mind, I work everything backwards. I start with where do I want my marriage to end up, where do I want my family to end up, where do I want my business looking, and then what are the things I can do to make that happen, how do I reverse engineer that? One of the core areas I think a lot of entrepreneurs miss on is they don't think about their profitability of each of the products and services they sell, they don't think about gross margin.

You need to be able to make money off of everything you do, which means you tend to need to listen to your customers and find out what they want to buy. I think, too often, we fall in love with our products and services and try to sell something that nobody needs. That's really one of the reasons why I started the COO Alliance. There's literally an infinite number of groups for entrepreneurs, but no one is doing anything to help the second-in-command.

Mike Agugliaro:
Yeah. That makes sense. Also, if the listeners profit first. Right? Mike McCall is another good friend and mentor of mine. I agree, Cameron. Why don't people even think about profit anyway? I don't even know why people think like, let me make money but I have nothing left.

Do you think this is another grandparent thing handed down to us?

Cameron Herold: I'm not sure. I mean, there's definitely been a tilt over the last 20 years, because of a lot of the VC funded companies and people with burn rates and people investing for the future. That's again going against what grandmother told us, which is, don't put all your eggs in one basket. I think people need to take money out of their business every year and use that to invest in real estate, to invest in their future, to invest in retirement, instead of plowing it all back in against growth. I think, too often, entrepreneurs are also focused on revenue, revenue, revenue. Revenue is kind that like badge, but it's not ...

I laugh at entrepreneurs who, I did $8 million in revenue. I'm like, really? How much did you take out last year? $300,000. Big deal. I can show you how to run a million dollar business and make $800,000, but what's the point. People need to focus on the revenue, they need to focus on profit, they need to focus on customer engagement, employee engagement, and then strategically, where they are growing the company. I think, too often, we become too maniacal or too focused on just about one number of revenue.

Mike Agugliaro: Yeah. I was caught in that same trap, too. I mean, when we probably just started to figure out that how important really paying attention to profit was when maybe we were doing $20 million. I mean, this year, we're on track for 32. I would tell you, profit is an ongoing conversation. It's something we look at, it's something we pay attention to, and it's something we have to question. If we're unhappy with it, you know, what parts of the business are causing that kind of virus of unhappiness in profits, so that's an amazing point. Cameron, at this point, people are saying, okay, cool, how do I find out more about Cameron, what he's got going on, what he's doing? Where should they go?

Cameron Herold: Yeah. The easiest place is to get, obviously, the books. You can get it at Amazon, or Double Double is also available on Audible and iTunes, but both Meetings Suck and Double Double are available in hardcopy and in Kindle format. They can get any of my videos for my speaking events. They can get those … or any of my worksheets, they can get those at CameronHerold.com. Then otherwise, they can find out information about the COO Alliance just by going to the COOAlliance.com.

Mike Augugliaro: Awesome. Cameron, I cannot thank you enough for delivering all this amazing content, information to everybody. Thank you for being a friend and a mentor. I respect you so much. You're serving so many people. Keep up the good work. Thank you.

Cameron Herold: Mike, love to help, being on the show and I'm super proud of what you guys are building with your core business to [inaudible 00:50:07], and also what you're doing with your warrior stuff as well. You're really changing lives out there, so it's pretty cool stuff. Thanks for having me.

Mike Augugliaro: Thank you. There you have it, everybody. You know and I'm going to go fast and furious on this. All the gold nuggets here, you will have to listen to this over and over again. In the meantime, before you're even done, just do what I did. Go to Amazon, order a bunch of books, go to Cameron Herold's website. Look, a couple of great golden nuggets, right? Meetings don't suck, we suck at running meetings. Guess what? Train your employees how to run the meeting and have a clear purpose for the meeting, three outcomes. Have a clear agenda, right? What order, how long are we going to cover each item?

He did so nice, right? Purpose, outcome, agenda. I mean, it's a nice structure. Book your meeting for half the time, I'll be doing that with the meeting I have this week, and start those meetings on time. Just like this, so here, we'll end five minutes early. I love that we put me right through the structure. Make sure you got a moderator for those meetings. Guess what? Get your people in line.

Give them all the books, talk about how to do it, get things aligned. What about the strategic thinking system, right? Get alone, grab a notepad. What are your goals first? What are your projects and things you could do to make this even happen? Guess what? Vote on the ones that are the easiest, and guess what, get to action on it.

Then he talked about daily huddles, and guess what, the CEOs should speak last. I'm going to do some testing in that myself and do what the best do. Momentum creates, guess what, momentum. Don't start with delegation, create clarity and vision, and the list goes on and on. Don't fear the creative tension. That was a big golden nugget. How about this? Your network is your net worth. Boom! That's a quote from Cameron Herold right there. Delegate everything but your genius. I think you tied a nice bow and ribbon around this. Ask yourself, where do you want to end up on all levels, family, business, health?

That's it of this episode of the CEO Warrior Show. I'd be grateful if you'd rate my show in iTunes. That helps me tremendously. We're keeping it visible so we could serve other people to change and have a better life and better business. I'd be very grateful if you did that. Be sure to connect with me on social media. It is a great way to ask me any questions and offer feedback. Until next time. Remember, massive wealth, tons of freedom and market domination is only one action step away.

Key Lessons Learned:

Meetings
- Meetings don't suck, we suck at running meetings.
- People just need the basic skills to make meetings more successful.
- Every meeting has to have a clear purpose. One sentence.
- Every meeting has to have clear outcomes and a clear agenda.
- Book every meeting for half the time you initially think you need.

- Every meeting should start on time. Stop your meetings five minutes early.
- Get a copy of <u>Meetings Suck</u> for your team and get them to read it.
- Engagement can be seen in the small details like how punctual someone is, whether they offer ideas to improve, they show genuine interest, or taking initiative.
- People don't understand the time constraints on meetings, write down interruptions and deal with them later. Have a moderator to keep things on topic.
- Follow these rules and your team will begin to fall in line.
- Every company should have a yearly retreat to establish goals, a quarterly retreat for the leadership, monthly meetings for strategic thinking and metric reviews. A daily huddle for the whole company can be helpful as well.
- The CEO or leader should be the one to speak last. Let the team figure stuff out first.

Strategic Thinking

- Just do what the best companies do, they've already figured it out.
- Use the post it note system and choose your goals.
- Brainstorm on the projects that will get you moving towards your goals.
- Eliminate the projects that won't work.

Business Vision

- Don't start with delegation, start with inspiration.
- Tell your team what you want built instead of how to do it.
- Describe your company three years in the future as if it exists already. Document the vision in as much detail as possible so that your team can make it happen.
- Goals are not the vision, the experiences, customers, and operations should be the vision.
- Get away from technology and create a mind map, you will be surprised how much you will come up with.
- When you don't tell people what you're building, they will just assume you are trying to make tomorrow better.
- Figure out where you want to end up and then figure out a way to profit from your efforts so you can get there.

- Don't just focus on revenue and profit.

Fear
- The people you grew up with may not think the same way as you.
- The more you share your dreams the more people will conspire to make it happen.

Network
- The people you spend the most time with determine how much money you will make.
- Surround yourself with people that are at a higher level than you.
- Look for an accountability partner.

Second in Command
- Start with an executive assistant before you hire a second in command.
- Write down the top 5 things they need to get done in the first 12 months.
- A COO has to be someone you can get along with.
- Delegate everything that you don't love to do, look for someone who compliments your strengths.
- Entrepreneurs tend to train themselves to everything on your own.
- A lifestyle business is a business that can run without you, you can choose to create this.

Final Tips
- Train your employees on how to run meetings.
- Start them on time and end them early.
- Figure out your goals and how to achieve.
- Delegate everything except your genius.

Learn more at CameronHerold.com

Take Action!

___ Stop doing actions (Actions you currently do now but should stop doing)

_____

_____

___ Keep doing actions (Actions you currently do now and should keep doing)

_____

_____

___ Start doing actions (Actions you don't do now but should start doing)

_____

_____

___ Who will do new actions? (Assign the action to yourself or someone else)

_____

_____

___ By when? (When will these actions be complete?)

_____

_____

CONVERSATION WITH MIKE MICHALOWICZ

WHY ENTREPRENEURS SHOULD TAKE THEIR PROFIT FIRST

CEOWARRIOR.com/podcast-mike-michalowicz/

In this episode of the secrets of business mastery podcast, Mike Agugliaro interviews Mike Michalowicz, who is an entrepreneur, investor, and the author of Toilet Paper Entrepreneur and Profit First. During the show, Mike Michalowicz shares how to make massive profits and why everything you know about profit has been hurting you and not helping you.

Main Questions Asked:
- What is profit?
- Why should profit not be scary?
- What was your motivation behind writing the book *Profit First*?
- If people want to get more profit what do they have to keep in mind?
- Talk more about niches and the uber focus concept.
- What is the one thing business owners should think about and do today?

Mike Agugliaro:	Hello everybody and welcome to this episode of the CEO WARRIOR podcast. My name is Mike Agugliaro and this is the podcast dedicated to business owners. Teaching you how to fast track your business growth and give you practical, do-able tips that you can implement today. Grab your pen and notepad and let's get started.
	Today I'll be interviewing a good friend of mine, and mentor, Mike Michalowicz, about how to position yourself in the market today. The surge way. Let me tell you a little bit about Mike before we get started. He's a globally recognized, entrepreneurial advocate. He is the author of multiple business books including "Profit First", "the Pumpkin Plan", and newly released "Surge", and what Business Week declared an instant business cult classic, "The Toilet Paper Entrepreneur". He is a former small business columnist for the Wall Street Journal, small business makeover segment. Host on MSNBC and the entrepreneur behind three multi-million dollar companies. Without any further delay. Mike, how are you today?
Mike Michalowicz:	I'm doing good brother, how you doing?
Mike Agugliaro:	Good. I got to tell you, first off, I love your name. It's a really nice name. Not your last name, but like the "Mike" part, you know?
Mike Michalowicz:	Oh, it's kind of sexy. There was smart parents back in the 70's and 60's and 80's. They called us Mike.
Mike Agugliaro:	Yeah I agree. It's very good. Listen, what is the deal? There is all these people. I'm looking all over Social Media people like, The Surge, The Surge, The Surge and so why don't you just dig in a little bit. What the hell's this Surge thing?
Mike Michalowicz:	People are saying we're on the verge of the surge. What it is, I got an email from one of my readers. I've written three other books prior to Surge, and this person slapped me on the side of the head. Usually an email I get, thank

you for your book, and this has impacted me and people tell their story. This person said, I love your books, but ... and you hate seeing the word "but", but ... it's all wasted if I'm not in the right place at the right time. Meaning, you can follow the Profit First methodology, you can facilitate explosive growth using The Pumpkin Plan, but if the guy bringing out the typewriter today, you're in the wrong place at the wrong time. That was a good idea 50 years ago. Today, you got to be in computing technology. Keyboarding is the replacement for the typewriter. This person said the most important thing that no one talks about is being in the right place at the right time.

That was three years ago, I got it. I started researching it out. I created a thesis and I said, is it really possible ... Is there a magic bullet that we can position ourselves in the right place at the right time? If you think about it Mike, if you or I could predict the Stock Market just five minutes in advance, we could make a decision now, as to the right place at the right time for the moving of the market and we would literally be billionaires. It's a fascinating question.

My application of it is to small business. How can a small business position itself where the market is moving and capture that momentum. Here's the answer ... There is no magic bullet, but you can greatly increase the odds. "Surge" was my study of companies that have done it from UGG Boots to a company called Speck who made cases for the iPhone, to Chef Dominique Ansel, the guy who founded the Cronut. How did these people do it, and what's the formula. That's what Surge is all about.

Mike Agugliaro:	That's really awesome. Has this been something that people have already adopted, this strategy, into their companies and what are some examples of what's going on with this.
Mike Michalowicz:	The vast majority of businesses are reactive businesses, not proactive. Surge is about being proactive. I bet you most of these people listening in are saying, what do

customers need? What's the buzz in my industry? What kind of work needs to be done? I'm going to start chasing after that. I'm going to be a provider. That's too late for the surge. Most businesses, therefore, have to market very aggressively to get part of the business out there. The idea of surge is being in front of consumer demand and therefore, it actually reduces your need for marketing. If you can position yourself where you are one of the early adopters or early providers into a market, the grow in demand will supersede the supply, therefore you automatically get marketed by the customers. There isn't enough supply so people say, hey, where do you get this product, where do you get this offering, where do you get this service. People come to you.

Let me give you some examples. I'll start off with UGG because I think it's a fascinating story. I sat down with Brian Smith, the founder of UGG. It's not a billion dollar plus company. A lot of people don't know that UGG did not start out by selling as a fashion product. It was actually targeted specifically and exclusively for surfers. What Brian Smith did in 1979 when he founded UGG, he said, what's the big, eminent need in the surfing community. Why surfers? He was a surfer himself. He had moved from Australia to California to watch the surf scene and participate in it.

This is the key ... and by the way, Surge, the title of the book is the moving of a wave, but it's also an acronym. S U R G E stands for the five steps you need to take. The 1st step is at separate. "S" in Surge, stands for separate. What Brian Smith did, and every company that has surged, first picked out a very targeted niche consumer base, to observe their behavior.

People tell me, what's the big trend going on now. What's the opportunity? Well, there's thousands of opportunities. We have to first pick the place we're going to market to. Just finishing out the start of UGG's surge is Brian was now studying surfers. He's watching their behavior and a fascinating thing was happening in the

70's. It was the rise of neoprene, the sophistication of neoprene suits. Neoprene existed prior, but it was a thick, harder material, less flexible. Advances were taking place in neoprene allowing it to be thinner, yet retain body warmth, to be more flexible. What this meant, Mike, by 1979, is that now surfers could wear neoprene suites out into the water and comfortably surf, which meant, they could surf in colder weather.

Surfing used to be a summer sport effectively. Neoprene allowed it to be a year round sport. It changed the whole paradigm of surfing. Here's what Brian observed ... And this is the next stage of surge. "U", the 2nd step, stands for Unify. What is the common, new problem in a market that people are trying to address and how do you unify a solution to match that? Specifically, what happened to surfers, he observed that when they come in after a set out in the ocean, in the freezing Pacific Ocean in the winter, they will come out and their feet were freezing. They had to keep their feet exposed to grip onto the board so they would wrap them in blankets. They would try to get them near a fire pit on the beach, do anything to warm up their freezing feet. That's when it hit, oh my gosh, there's been a shift.

Any action will cause an equivalent and different reaction in the market place. The action of the creation and use of neoprene, caused a reaction of freezing feet in the winter. There was an opportunity here. Brian Smith, that then, brought about the UGG boot. You say, I got to get surfer's feet warm, and he brought the boot to the community. It was unexpected and new, but the early adopters were willing to try it out and willing to fudge through the resistance of the market. I can share more about that, but it's natural when you introduce something for a market that's new and unique, inevitably there will be some resistance from the people that are doing the traditional old way.

Mike Agugliaro:	I love that whole "Separate" part and how you piece that all together. I know a lot of business owners listening to this right now are going, "You know what? Yeah, maybe

I am reactive versus proactive, and maybe I'm not in front of the consumer demand. Maybe I am lagging." So, what's part two in this, the "U" of Surge.

Mike Michalowicz:

It stands for Unify. As they separate, the more specific your community, the more in tune you can be with what they need and therefore get in front of it. "U" stands for Unify. Unify is, what is the unifying need that the consumer base has? You have to observe the market. The reason most people don't get in front of the consumer demand is because we serve everybody and their mother. Therefore, there is no unifying need. This guy needs this, another customer needs that, we're constantly trying to address a one off basis. If you pick a very specific niche, we then see a unification around a need, a problem that's been arising.

Here's another example. Tony Lillios, the founder of Speck. Speck started off as a brand new startup out of a garage. Surpassed, I think, 50 million off to 250 million before he sold out of his interest in the business. When I was talking to Tony, a wonderful guy, he shared a fascinating story. He was a designer and saw the rise of mobile technology. Here's a shift in the market again. Every action, there is a reaction. He saw a shift in the market, sees the rise of phones, and says, what's this going to trigger for consumers. He walked into an AT&T store, back in the 90's, late 90's, and different phone stores, Version and so forth, and was watching the accessories they had. I don't know if you remember back then Mike, you'd walk into any Verizon or wireless store, all the cases were black. Fake leather, black cases. Hard plastic black ... everything was black. It was one color.

Remember this about history. History repeats. I don't know if you remember the automobile, but there was a time ... The story of the automobile, but Ford was the founder of the automobile, brought it to the US, starts manufacturing, in one color ... Black. Until, I think it was General Motors who came about and said we're going to offer a variety of colors. Changed the game forever. They got huge volumes of business by just adding color. Tony saw the same opportunity. History is repeating here in the phone market. I'm going to bring about some color. He was the first one to make a red case, then different case designs. Speck, as a result, grew explosively.

The lessons here at stage two is, once you've identified your separated group, find out the unifying problem or need they have. As customers come in, what's the thing that's frustrating them consistently. What are the early adopters trying to do. What Tony also noticed was, people were buying these black phone cases, the only kind you could get, and putting stickers on it and trying to give it some personality. The consumer was trying to do this on their own. He saw that he had an opportunity to provide this solution for them, right at the store itself.

Mike Agugliaro:	Mike, I don't want to go past the Unified part too quick. Do you think, or do you see today, because you're speaking in front of huge crowds, you're talking to business owners all the time. Do you see that the trend or the consumer need they're following, is just what they've been taught from maybe their competitors or what everybody else is doing?
Mike Michalowicz:	It's very common for businesses to copy the competition. Usually that puts you in a stage where you need to catch up. Sometimes the wave has passed. This Surge concept ... the analogy I run throughout the book is surfing. It's no coincidence, surfers go through the same experience. When a surfer is out in the ocean trying to surf, they don't look at waves that are way out on the horizon, they look for eminent waves. There is one lesson I need to get across in Surge, as people read it. You must look for what's eminent, there must be a movement that's proven to be taking hold. Then, once it's approaching us, we need to paddle in front of it to catch it. A lot of businesses say, oh my God, that other business has already caught the wave. Look at XYZ, my competitor, it's doing so and so. I need to do the same.

This is a paddle after the fact. Is it possible to catch up?

Yeah. Does the competitor have a massive advantage? Yeah, because they are ahead of you. They've learned. They have a lot of momentum on their side. In micro-niches, small communities, small pack- The guy who's the first mover has a massive advantage. It's in larger markets where the first mover doesn't have as much of an advantage because they have to blaze a trail.

A lot of people look at Uber for example and are like, wow. Being Lift, the #2 company in, ain't so bad. Uber has blazed the trail for Lift. They are fighting all the battles in court and Lift just kind of sweeps in behind them. Maybe it's good to be #2. That's generally true in large market movements, but in micro-niches ... I'm working just with bookkeepers, for example. That's the niche my company services. It's a micro community. It doesn't touch everyone in the world, it touches a very small community. First mover advantage is significant. We have to. If your business is under $100 million, or even under $500 million dollars in revenue, which I suspect is almost everyone listening to this call right now, you are serving a micro niche. Either it's a geographically based niche, a demographically based niche. It's definitely not all consumers. You have to get in front of the wave to have the biggest impact. Not try to be paddling behind and catching up.

Mike Agugliaro:	Mike, how do you even figure this out? I mean, some of these people are so deep in the weeds of their business they only know what they know. Is there a way to ... Is there something to look at? Is there a question that we should be asking ourselves? Is it, go meditate with a Monk? How do you really start to think like, okay, get ahead of the consumer need. What would you tell them?
Mike Michalowicz:	Two techniques. One is simply seek out the word traditional. This is the easy, quick research kind of technique. The traditional means, when you are working with your existing customers, observe and ask. What have you traditionally done? For me, I'll just give you an example in the bookkeeping space because that's the market I'm targeting. By the way, when I write my books,

I think I'm a kind of unique author. I don't just write a book of people I've studied. That's part of it, but I also try the techniques on my own businesses first. I started an organization called Profit First Professionals, using the Surge technique. What I did, I went and asked the bookkeepers, the market I decided to target, and I started saying, what's bookkeeping been like traditionally? When you start finding a pattern for tradition ... I'll tell you one thing, tradition is always the thing on the way out, and is being replaced by new.

There used to be traditional clothes. No one wears those any more. There used to be traditional way ... Traditionally, the way music was created, that no longer happens. Look for tradition and know that's the thing on the way out. Of course, the question is, what's the thing replacing it? Here's what you've got to look for. It's the early adopters, also known as the cool kids. Here's a great example. The electric car. If you and I are talking about the electric car, even five years ago, ten years ago, we'd laugh and say we were talking about a golf cart. Today, the electric car is Tesla and other cars like Leaf from Nissan, so forth. It's really the Tesla that's taking hold.

We know this is an eminent wave. There is a rise to the electric car. It's extremely important to observe because there is an opportunity here and we know it because the early adopters have fought through the original resistance. Here's what happens in any [inaudible 00:17:19] why, as tradition dies out, a new replacement comes about. The early adopters say "Oh, I want to try out that new Tesla." Then, the people that's around them attack them for making bad decisions. Are you crazy, you bought an electric car? Think about five years ago, even ten years ago. An electric car was a golf cart, there was no alternative. It's too weak in power. If you get an impact ... Remember the conversations of only five years ago. If a Tesla crashes there's going to be battery acids and an explosion. It's going to be the most devastating accident of all time, which now we know, not to be true.

In all these different attacks, the question is this. Can the early adopters have enough fortitude to stick through the attack and the resistant. Meaning, do they continue to do it. Then you start seeing a turning point. When the early adopters stick with it and now the emulators, the 2nd stage, kicks in and buys it. You know the emulators exist when you start seeing it, with the Tesla, in your own neighborhood. Chances are Mike, you've seen Tesla's driving around, maybe you know someone that owns one. Maybe you own one. I see them drive around my neighborhood. This means it's taking foot hold and now the surge is starting to grow. Tesla just got 400,000 orders, the most orders in history for an automobile. We know there is an eminent opportunity.

I'm not saying the opportunity is electric cars. What I'm saying is, what are all the reverberating, ripple effects that are going to come off of this. Electric cars, they use a lot of energy for cooling and heating. Can someone create a new interior material, or windshield material that will reduce the drain of cooling and heating, maybe control the temperature. What about fueling stations? Massive opportunity potentially coming our way. New tires and stuff. Different products for these cars. Maybe new driving schools. Maybe electric cars, maybe drivers ed is going to start shifting. There is a lot of similarities, but there's some differences.

The key is this, we all must look for what's eminent by saying, are the cool kids doing it and are they sticking with it. What was traditional that's going away? Are gasoline automobile cars, that's the tradition, everyone has the gasoline car. Tradition fades, early adopters that sticks with it, show something that's new. Once we identify these two, start asking yourselves, what does this mean? What's the opportunity? How can I serve this market? Keep asking yourself and then start testing it out in that market and you'll be in front of the surge.

Mike Agugliaro:
You know what I like about that? Is this true? Sometimes the surge will start and if you notice the surge that someone else started, can you surpass them, just by

being a little more strategic?

Mike Michalowicz:	Oh yeah. The Surge, this is a wave that's eminent. Meaning, it's not cresting when the best ride happens. Right now, there's the wave. If you ever watch surfers out there, a huge massive wave can get 20 surfers on it. There is all the kind of different areas the waves carve up. Like I said, with the electric car, there is everything from cabin control to tire manufacturing, to drivers ed, to fueling stations, to all these different opportunities. We're still at the beginning. It hasn't crested.

Let me give you a comparative, just so you know, of a wave that's premature. Also in the automobile space, there's a lot of talk about autonomous cars. Google is putting research into it. I think Facebook has invested in autonomous cars. Everyone is saying the next big thing is autonomous cars. Let's be cautious about that. That's a wave out in the horizon and it's not ride able yet. Here's the test ... Who are the cool kids using autonomous cars right now? How many autonomous cars have you seen in your neighborhood? Probably none. Do you know anyone that owns one? No. Therefore, the wave is not eminent. It hasn't got to that early adopter test, therefore, maybe it's a cool idea but if you start working in that market it's way early and you're not going to catch the opportunity.

Conversely, we can look at hybrid cars. Hybrid cars are established. That's a wave that has passed. Does it show momentum? Yes. Is there still an opportunity to ride it? Yeah, but it's not a surging wave. Here's the difference between a wave that's too early, too late, and surging. A surging wave means that demand is increasing at an exponential rate and supply is growing at a linear rate. That means, as demand grows at a rate of ten times, supply may be only growing at a rate of one times. What happens in a scenario like that, is that, because there is less supply than demand, consumers will seek you out. They will go to extraordinary measures to find you. I now have an electric car. I need to find a fueling station for example. I will start asking friends. I will go to extraordinary measure to find where can I get this car fueled up. If you have a fueling station, electrical charging station, you have a massive opportunity right now.

Here's one of the dangers, Mike. If demand outstrips supply, marketing is less important because people will go to extraordinary measures to find you. You'll think that you're a genius because all these people are flocking to you. You get leads left and right, business is flowing in. Then you're like, see? I don't even need a market I'm so good. The answer is, no, you're not that good. You just have something that everyone wants and no one else has done it yet. This means that you actually need to jump on production. You need to improve what you're doing. It's only a matter of time before competition starts expanding and you better be prepared for that. You need to improve ... When you have lots of leads coming in, it doesn't mean to just ride that wave and do nothing. You have to start improving your offering dramatically because it's only a matter of time before the competition steps in.

Mike Agugliaro:	I always say something like, success is a gift and a curse, right? It's a gift because you're now successful. It's a curse because a lot of successful people become complacent and then before you know it, someone else has stomped on your space. What is the "R" now, after the Unify?
Mike Michalowicz:	It stands for Rally cry. What Rally cry is, is the message that protects the early adopters. It allows them to fight through the resistance that they're going to feel. It's the unifying filter that invites in the consumers you want and filters out the ones you don't. A Rally cry is like a mission statement. It's an easy message for those consumers to convey. Not just consumers, it can be clients, it can be for a service based business. I have a service based business. For example, in my company, Profit First Professions, who serves bookkeepers, our message, our Rally cry is, "Eradicate Entrepreneurial Poverty". That's simply our mission. We exist to eradicate entrepreneurial

poverty. Most entrepreneurs are impoverished. Most entrepreneurs live check by check, regardless of the size of their business, they're not taking home any money. Our goal is to eradicate that. For the right consumer, they get it. It connects with them. For the wrong consumer for us, they have no idea what we're talking about, so it becomes a filter.

The early adopters who say okay, I'm going to belong to Profit First Professionals. Now, when they get attacked by the community around them because we're very early to the market, we're trying to ride a surge here and the other people say this is stupid, what's this Profit First thing that you're doing. They say, hey, this business ... Why I'm involved with it is because we are eradicating entrepreneurial poverty. Here's perhaps an even better example. With UGG, when the first surfer was walking down the beach with these spies like us, crazy, big boots, that person looked like a total odd ball. I can only imagine that the surfers back in the 70's were laughing their ass off because someone was wearing these boots around the beach. No one had ever done that before. That surfer then had the rally cry which was, "No more cold feet" or "year round surfing". He says listen, I can surf year round now man, my feet are never cold. That powerful, simple rally cry converted the 2nd stage of people, the emulator, to say, oh, I get it. They start buying it and that's where the momentum really started exploding.

Mike Agugliaro:	I love that. I can see how it plays out from the part you already said, "separate" ... Market in that different place. Then "unify" and now there's "rally cry" the message that not only protects the followers, but keeps the momentum moving. What is the "G" part?
Mike Michalowicz:	It stands for "Gather". That's why I acknowledge back to Rally cry. You're a Warrior CEO, you have the rally cry is, you're warriors. You're in the fight of a lifetime here. It's such a clear message. Look at the organization you've grown as a result. Every business needs to have that.

"G" stands for gather. Gather is when you're surfing in the actual ocean and you're up on a wave, the rally phase is kind of where the wave converts over to energy starts carrying you. It's interesting in surfing that you have to paddle. You have to exert all this energy to get the momentum of the wave but now, once you're up on the wave, everything you do changes. From exerting energy to now capturing energy. Adjust your balance and movements to get what's called the pocket of the wave. The pocket is the heart of the wave. It's where the most force is exerted and if you can get there you will get the fast, strongest, best ride.

In business, once we have a rally cry, it means we've got the inaugural group carrying us, we in our business, very quickly need to find the pocket. What's the core actions of this movement we've captured. In fact, my own business Profit First Professionals, we're there. We have the early members who have rallied around us. We have people that love our organization and now our job is to find out what is the heart of what is impacting them so we can ride that.

Gathering means, once you've got a little momentum with your consumer base, ask them. Why are you buying from me? What am I doing right? What do I need to do to amplify it? Keep understanding it. Tweak your offering. This is the concept that was written about by Eric Ries in Lean Startup. He talks about the minimal viable product. A basic core offering will get us through the first three stages "SUR", but now we need to start enhancing the product. Our customers know what the answer needs to be and we have to pay absolute attention to it and respond to it accordingly.

One of my favorite examples, my daughter is going to college next year. She is going to Virginia Tech and in the heart of Virginia Tech ... I even wrote about this in the book. In the heart of Virginia Tech, on the campus, is what they called the Drill Field. It's the main field where students that are staying in dormitories have to cross to get to their classrooms. On there, the school smartly put sidewalks to walk to the classrooms. The unsmart thing was they didn't pay attention to what the customer ... the customers, or looking at what the students were really doing. They didn't gather. What happened was when the sidewalks were installed, then within a year or two there was these trails that the students had blazed because they walked the most direct route from their dorm room to the classroom and it wasn't on these paths. It was their own paths.

What Virginia Tech should have done was watch what the student does, the consumer. Then make the paths after the fact. Observe the customers behavior and then make it very easy for them. Now that you're offering to a very specific community, you have a very specific need you're catering to, there's a big rally around it, pay very, very, very close attention to your customer. Make adjustments in your service or your product to match up to what they're doing on their own.

Brian Smith, the founder of UGG, he knows that when surfers walked down the beach, that sand was kicking up into their boots. They were trying to prevent the sand from coming in, even duct taping the top of the boot to keep it tight. What he did is simply raise the boot. When you walk down ... there's a reason UGGs are so high, calf high, so when you walk down the beach, sand doesn't kick into your boot. You have to constantly gather knowledge, observe your customers and then respond accordingly.

Mike Agugliaro:	I love it. Just that piece alone, if you just think, inside your own business, just for a couple of minutes. Magic will come out of it, because it really is. Gathering to adjust as needed to be in that sweet spot. Mike, do you see a lot of people, they get in the sweet spot ... I'm thinking, and it's funny, like Yellow Pages just came to my mind for some reason. I still use Yellow Pages to market but the sweet spot was, if you were big enough, brave enough and bold enough to be the largest in Yellow Pages, this was a real sweet marketing spot. It's like, "Who moved my cheese"? People thought it would

never change and then the company stopped.

Mike Michalowicz:	It's so funny. The Yellow Pages just ... the old book was thrown on my driveway just a few days ago. Literally, just a couple of days ago. The truck came by throwing the Yellow Pages, which is one tenth the size it used to be ... on my driveway. I picked it up and said to my wife, when was the last time you read the Yellow Pages? She was like, I didn't even know they still made it. We threw it right into our recycle. I then ... This is the gathering thing. Once you see a behavior in yourself, ask others. I literally walked down the street, it was the weekend. Many of my neighbors were out. I said, hey did you get the Yellow Pages? I said, what did you do with it? They said, threw it out. Everybody threw it out. That is a strong indicator that it is going away. But, people cling on to tradition, something we talked about earlier. I've always done the Yellow Pages, it's always worked so well for me. I'm going to continue to do it. That's tradition. Tradition is on the way out. I suspect if I'd leafed through there, the biggest ads are the people that aren't redirecting that money towards Social Media, toward online marketing, toward other opportunities, even billboard or real time marketing. Those people, I question if their business is going to sustain if they stay stuck in tradition.
Mike Agugliaro:	I agree with you, especially if they stay in that tradition. We're working with some company, 1901, 1906, 1930, and man, the old school traditions that they just don't want to let go of. They still think it's like doing business the good ole boy's way. The good ole boys didn't have a cellphone, maybe they had two Styrofoam cups with a string. It's just different today. What is the ... Tie us up with the "E" here.
Mike Michalowicz:	"E" stands for Expand. I'm always hesitant to talk about this phase because so many people, Mike, jump "S-U-R-G" they skip those phases, and say, I just want to expand baby, expand. If you don't master the first four steps, expansion will never actually happen. Here's what

expansion is. Once you identify what's working in the first four stages, the niche you've targeted, the unifying need that's occurred, the rally cry you've built around that, and the gathering of knowledge. Once you've done this, you now replicate that model out to a larger base of customers that have the exact same sequence of needs.

Best explain is to give an example. Brian Smith, UGG. He's targeting a surfer. That's where he started in 1979. He started getting serious traction, took him far into the process. It took him about, ten years to get traction. Once he had traction, he then analyzed what worked. Here's what he found. He said that for surfers, when he created a new UGG, a boot, that he initially marketed it through models. He'd hire male and female models to show off the boots, but that wouldn't cause sales. In fact, surfers would look at those models and say those are posers, man, they're not real surfers. Why should I ever buy his boots? He did find though that semi-pro athletes, the semi-pro surfers, when they wore the boots, everyone wanted to be like the semi-pros or the pros. He got the boots on them and then saw that really started to explode.

Then he said to himself, this is working for athletes who get cold feet and copy the pros and semi-pros, what other markets are like this? He said, well, hockey players get cold feet after coming off the ice and they're sweaty and stuff. Skiers have this issue. Hunters in the winter ... Who are the semi-pros and pros in those markets? He went and marketed to those groups. Got the semi-pro and pro hockey players, the pro skiers. Got them wearing the boots and it exploded.

Then, and only then, he was well past the $100 million dollars in revenue. I think he was at $200 million dollars in revenue, he said what's the biggest, most competitive, most cut throat market out there. Everyone knows it's teenage girls. They're insanely intense. He said, if I can get the pro teenage girls, so to speak, to wear these boots, I wonder if the same thing will happen. His breakthrough moment happened in early 2000 where he got Brooke Shields to wear UGG boots, cover of People Magazine, or US Weekly, and all of a sudden, every teenage girl needed to wear these boots. They went from 100's of millions to billion plus in revenue.

Mike Agugliaro: That's amazing when you think about ... I can see what you're saying. I can see in my industry a lot, people want to expand into other trades which might be good but if you suck at your one thing that you're doing and you don't have ... You're going to suck at ... You'll suck more when you compound, adding more things to a crappy system, right?

Mike Michalowicz: Oh my God, yeah. I'm a co-owner in a manufacturing business and this is the lesson I got from manufacturing. I've learned so much by my life in manufacturing, the next book I'm working on is taking these principals, because the realization of every business, your business, my business, we're all manufacturers. We all go through a sequence of steps to generate an end product. In our case, a service based businesses. Usually an emotion, we want people to feel confident, or happy, or stress free. Whatever the emotion is, but we have to manufacturer it. Well, the lesson from manufacturing is this. You identify the end product you want to make. You reverse engineer the sequence to get there, and you figure out how to do it with the fewest steps and the least waste. You also know the more variables you have, the more steps, the likelihood of disaster happening, increases expediently.

In service based businesses we want to do the same thing. Reduce the number of things we need to do. You can only do that by reducing the type of customer set. If you view the same customer with the same need, over and over, it's the same sequence of steps you have to go through, you can master it. If we broaden out our customer base and broaden out our service set, you better be real good because now there are a lot of variables you need to juggle. That's the problem with expansion. Most businesses, Mike, start the expansion phase when they're not even a million dollars in revenue. They're trying to do everything for everybody right away.

You haven't even mastering manufacturing one thing yet and you're trying to expand. Master one thing. That's the "S-U-R-G" phase. Once you've truly mastered it, replicate that formula through new products or services, but only when you've mastered the first one.

Mike Agugliaro:	That's incredible, all put together. Let's dive in to ... Is there anything else on the Surge concept that you feel the listeners need to know before I jump into just some general questions about some stuff?
Mike Michalowicz:	One last thing. When I talk about this, people say, I don't know if I want to be the next UGG, I mean, it sounds great but a billion dollar company is not who I am. It doesn't even fit my lifestyle. I don't want to be the big corporate guy speaking with investors all the time. I want to stay small but I want to be rich. I want to stay manageable, but I want to be wealthy. Surge mentality is only for big companies. The danger of sharing stories like UGG and Speck, if you've heard of that company. I use those names because everyone can recognize those names and maybe relate to it. Maybe your daughter has an UGG boot or maybe you've seen them in the market place.

I want to share one more story from the book that speaks to the guy who wants to ride the wave to a very healthy business but keep it small. It's the story of Chef Dominique Ansel. He is the founder of the Cronut. I don't know if you've ever heard of the Cronut. This was explosive success about five to seven years ago. He was the baker who found a way to blend a croissant with a doughnut and made this really unique pastry.

He was based out of New York City, he finds the Cronut demand skyrockets. Every newspaper, magazine, it's even on the news. CNN reports about this cool pastry that people are crazy to get. He's approached by major investors and they say, hey, why don't you open 100 of these stores. Why don't you have the Cronut phenomenon, we'll have it everywhere? And he said, no, that's not who I am or what I want. I want to stay one store. I want wild success, but I want to stay one store.

Today, six or seven years later, you can go any morning to downtown New York City, in the financial district. You can go to his bakery, Chef Dominique Ansel's bakery and you'll see, before it opens, 5:00 or 6:00 in the morning, a line forming to get his Cronut. Literally, sometimes the doors open there's 100 people waiting to get a Cronut. People have traveled the globe to get there. They're traveling through the city and this is a must see stop and experience. He's doing very well for himself, but he played it by his rules. The lesson is, you don't have to pick the size that you think your business needs to be. You can let the right size find you. This Surge process applies to any type of business, including the Cronut.

Mike Agugliaro:	That's awesome. You know what I was thinking, when you wrote that, it was like you've got to really control your mindset and don't sabotage your future because ... I don't know if you've ever heard this Mike, but people will go, you know ... I haven't heard it in a while but I used to hear it years ago. There's more to life than money, Mike. I would say, perfectly well said from a broke ass person.
	Maybe there is more to life than money, but money helps create a lot of amazing things. Not only for your life, if you're satisfied, why don't you play bigger so you can serve, maybe a charity. The other thing is, and someone did just say this the other day on one of my post in Social Media or whatever. They said, I don't want a bigger company, I like a small company because a small company is small problem. I disagree. If you keep telling yourself, "I like a small company, I like a small company", like you said, you want to grow. How is your mind ever going to find the strategy when you're like "I want to stay small, I want to stay small". Does that make sense?
Mike Michalowicz:	I'll tell you, whoever said a bigger business is a better business, is a total jerk off. Is a total jerk. Bigger ... But it

is the mindset Mike. So many people are like, how big is your business? You're only doing seven million, I'm doing 12 million, I'm better than you. All I care about is how much money I'm taking home. Let me tell you this. I believe money is extremely important because it reduces stress. I'll tell you what the top line is. The top line is stress points. My biggest business was a seven million dollar business. My smallest was zero dollars, from startup. As my businesses grew, the bigger the business, the bigger the payroll, the bigger the rent, the bigger all these different variables.

I knew in my seven million dollar company, I had a payroll. I remember my payroll was over $200 thousand, almost $300 thousand dollars a month in payroll. I remember sitting at home shaking, in sweats, in the middle of the night, saying, oh my God, if I can't get a big project this month I can't pay payroll. I can't refinance my house for a third time, there is no money left. It was beyond stressful. The top line of revenue is vanity. The bottom line profit is sanity. I am way more impressed Mike, by a business that does two million dollars in revenue and the owner is taking home $500,000 than a business that does seven million and the guy is taking home $150,000.

I want to know, how healthy is your business? In fact, I'm in these different entrepreneurial organizations and so forth. When I meet an entrepreneur it's always the "how big is the", question always comes up. Hey, how many employees have you got? How much revenue you doing? What do your sales look like? My response is tell me how healthy your business is. People are like, what do you mean how healthy? Tell me your bottom line, how healthy is it? What's the take home there? How profitable are you? They'll be like, I don't know.

It kills me. Why do we just focus on size alone. The Surge process we went over, yes, you can grow a very large business. You can grow the right size business for you but by being in front of consumer demand, it definitely positions you for the most profitable business.

When people want what you have and you're the only guy supplying it, trust me, there are massive profits there.

Mike Agugliaro:	Just so you know, I was going to say like, what she said, like 12 times during that, what you're saying there. You're so 100% correct on this. How many people have a big company, they think they're successful but they are divorced. Or, they think they're successful and they got diabetes. They are 200 pounds overweight or they think they are successful and their kids can't stand them. They think they're successful and they've totally alienated themselves from their family and being able to serve their family and there is no family time. I agree with you, I'm like, what's the health of your business, what's the health of your life, what is the level of your happiness.

It's funny, my son, when he was really little ... I don't know where we were driving, maybe we were driving to the zoo. We were going somewhere. He seen a homeless guy. This homeless guy was not a guy with a sign, my son was ... We were probably even assuming he's homeless. Probably because he wasn't super shaven or clean. He was just ... I had a conversation with my son and he was thinking like, look at this guy, right? I'm like, well here's the question that we don't know, is he homeless or is he free? One man might say to himself ... I know, studying a lot of religions with spiritual gurus and all that stuff, there is a couple of things. You can own material things or the material things can own you. Maybe that guy is like, I've got no worries, I'm free, there's no bills, there's no stress, or he could be [inaudible 00:45:14] and really suffering. You don't know until you ask a question.

Mike Michalowicz:	I think the lesson in there, that I hear is, we have to define success for ourselves first and then make it happen. I'll tell you, we should not, cannot, placate to what we believe societal success is. I bought into it initially. Bigger is better. That makes me happy, I want to be the big guy. I was pushing everything I could to grow my business and I hated every minute of it, the stress it caused. Now, I'm totally of this mind set. Let the right size find me. I have 30 employees. I was hoping to get 35

by the end of the year, for what? Now, five or six family members and my company is a million times better than that size. We have to define what our success is and then allow the business to naturally fill in around it as effectively as possible and as profitably as possible. I'm a huge believer in profit. That's where sustainability is. that's where comfort is. When a company has tons of money that it's sitting on, when those dark periods happen, and they happen for every business, you can get through them a lot easier when you're backed with cash.

Mike Agugliaro:	I think, you know ... Challenge the norm. This probably will freak some people out. Hopefully my employees aren't listening to it, but like, we're at 190 employees. I want to get to 175, but I want them all running like Spartans and I don't want a lot of waste and stuff. When you're just in the norm, I can tell you, you're justifying a lot of poor performance, poor attitude, poor results. The word that keeps coming back to me, Mike, and I'm curious what the word means to you. Especially in the manufacturing, it's "optimize". Optimize what the hell you're doing for the next level. What does that word, optimize, mean to you?
Mike Michalowicz:	Looking back at manufacturing, we're following a process called Lean Manufacturing. We've been two years since implementing this process and it is hard. The concept of Lean means there is accountability throughout. There is no passing the buck. In manufacturing this is true optimization, meaning ... In manufacturing as a product goes on, it actually becomes more costly. There's part of the problem. If, in the first step when I cut out the leather, or other manufacturer, and there's a problem, we lose the leather. If in the final step and we're about to go to the product and someone scrapes it with the razor and puts a slice into it, now the product which was sold for $350.00 has all the products invested in it, the parts, but also all the time put into.

Every step along the path, if the mistake happens, it becomes more costly. To optimize it, every person must be absolutely critical of the step that they are delivering and the step that came before them. There is constant quality checks built in. I believe this is in a service based business too. The sooner we detect a problem, the better. If we detect a problem, then we have to have the accountability to resolve it, fix it. Maybe we can do it by ourselves as an individual, maybe we can do the team, but we have to fix it. If that problem keeps on occurring, well now we're just ignoring a problem. To me optimization, again is, being critical of every single step and realizing that quality of service or quality of product doesn't happen at the end. It's not measured then, it must be measured every step of the way through and now become optimized. Less problems after you're done.

Mike Agugliaro:
I love the Lean Manufacturing part. I'm going to hit you with two last questions before we close out this show. One marketing question ... What do you think is a marketing avenue today that people should think about that either they are not tapping into or just something that you feel everybody should know about marketing a business today?

Mike Michalowicz:
I got to learn more about Facebook marketing. I'm late to that surge. I just started doing it and the impact is so powerful. The reason is, because of its specificity, meaning I can say, I want to market to a bookkeeper who is in Northern New Jersey, has read one of my books in the past and is at least five years in the business. I can whittle it down so specifically, literally I can pick out the perfect customer. The marketing opportunity is this ... You have to have your avatar for your perfect customer. If you don't have that, what weed have you been smoking? You've got to know who your perfect customer is, then target them. For me, Facebook is that now. For one thing, Facebook may not be where your best customers are congregating, maybe there is some other form but for many businesses, I'm finding that Facebook has perfect customers on there and it allows you to target that specific avatar. That's my marketing tip. Hit Facebook with your avatar.

Mike Agugliaro:	The last big question is ... You walk out in front of a million business owners today and you have to tell them something they should really think about over the next two to three years. What would you tell everybody?
Mike Michalowicz:	I do that, every single day. I mean, literally every single day. I'm speaking tonight. I've done it at your events now four or five times. You ask me, hey Mike, you want to come back and present, you want to give something fresh? No, I want to do the same thing because there's going to be new people there or people that don't believe me yet and I want to shake them like crazy and say wake up and take your profit first. I'm saying this until I'm blue in the face. I will not stop saying it. On my tombstone it's going to say, "Goddammit, take your profit first".
	Here's the concept Mike, I don't care how big or new, or old, or small your business is, every time there is cash coming in, every sale you make, you must take your profit first. Take a percentage and hide it away from your business. Profit is not an event. Not just going to happen one day, dammit it happens now. It is a habit. It must be baked into your business. Until you start doing this, you can never run a business as profitably as you can because you're always waiting for a profit to happen some day. Every business, millions of them, I'm hoping one day every one is touched by this message. Take your profit first and you'll be blown away by the improvements of your business and the profitability you'll have.
Mike Agugliaro:	Maybe what you need to do is get a big pair of boots, like cowboy boots or something, and on the bottom, stamp "Profit First" and if they don't listen you foot them in the forehead and all of a sudden they've got this imprint of Profit First. You would look very cool kicking your foot in someone's face, so that would be awesome.
Mike Michalowicz:	I kind of like that.
Mike Agugliaro:	I'm going to hold you to getting that done now. How do people ... They've listened to this, Mike, and they're all

jacked up now, Surge, Profit. How do they find out more about you?

Mike Michalowicz:
As you know, I've devoted my life now to serving small businesses. I do it through my books, so I have four books out there. The easiest way to learn about them and to improve your business, is go to MikeMichalowicz.com. Here's the deal, it's the longest, most polish name on the planet. I can't even spell the freaking thing, so there is two shortcuts. One is my nickname in high school is Mike Motorbike, so just type in MikeMotorbike.com, that will get you to me. The 2nd shortcut is, if you want to go for my full name, go to Google, type in Mike, M I K E. Then Mic, M I C, and by that point, the longest, most Polish sounding name that drops down, that's me.

Go there, it brings you to my website. All my books, there is free chapter downloads. You have no excuse. You can get this stuff for free, except you have to take action. That's the only question. Go to the site and get the free book downloads. I used to write for the Wall Street Journal for a few years. My best, most popular articles are up there, and if nothing else, I also do promise, this site is like no site you have ever visited. It'll be the most different site you've ever been to.

Mike Agugliaro:
What I'm going to do Mike, is I'm going to do something I've never done before. Anybody who attends my next event that Mike is going to be at, I'm going to let him share the story of how he defeated me. 31 years in martial arts, 8th degree black belt, developed my own system, and Mike Michalowicz defeated me and I'm going to let him share that at my next event. Well, Mike, I can't thank you enough for being on this podcast, for being an amazing friend and a mentor. Thank you so much today.

Mike Michalowicz:
It was an absolute joy, Mike. It always is. Thank you.

Mike Agugliaro:
There you have it everybody. You know we don't leave without some big Warrior Nuggets, so I'm going to run

through these really quick. First, be on the Verge of the Surge, and he did a great job of explaining what the Surge is. Be proactive and not reactive. And guess what? Be in front of the consumer demand. What about the Surge acronym? Separate - market in a different place. Unify - what is the unified need the consumer needs. Rally Cry - the message that protects the followers. Gather - adjust as needed to be in that sweet spot, change quick, enhance always. Expand - master the four steps first, then you can replicate that profit.

Then he gave us a whole bunch of other golden nuggets that we talked about. Don't sabotage your mind, don't be saying I like small or I'm okay. Always be prepared for the competition. I love this part that he said, it reminds me also, challenge the tradition. Also, define your success for yourself first before anything else. How about Lean Manufacturing? Accountability throughout the company. That's a great golden nugget for all of us to focus on. Social Media marketing, get your ass on it today. Make sure you have your perfect customer, perfect avatar. Target them. Last but not least, and I know Mike is going to get a big ass boot with Profit First on the bottom. Take your damn profit first because if anything, you deserve it.

That's it for this episode of the CEO Warrior podcast. I'd also be grateful if you'd rate my podcast on iTunes. It helps me tremendously with keeping my podcast visible so people who have never heard it can discover it. If you've already done this, thank you so much, I'm very grateful be sure to connect with me on Social Media. Yes, go to there now. It's a great way to ask me any questions or offer me feedback on the show. I'm also reachable at MikeA@CEOwarrior.com. Until next time remember, mass of wealth, tons of freedom, and market domination is only one action step away. Now, go take some damn profit.

Key Lessons Learned:

Traditional Profit Model
- Traditional GAP accounting profit formula: Sales – Expenses = Profit
- The issue with the above formula is that profit is an 'after thought' and is logical, but doesn't match human behavior.
- The formula we believe we should follow for profit is wrong.
- The definition of profit is the money leftover in your business at the end of a period of time. It is often a quarterly distribution of cash that solely benefits the owners of the business.
- Profit is cash in hand and not money you plow back into your business. Using it that way is simply a delayed expense.
- From an accounting perspective, when you have a profit, there is a threat of tax liabilities. The more money your business creates the more taxes you owe.

Profit First Model
- Profit First is a 'pay yourself first' concept.
- The formula is Sales – Profit = Expenses.
- Take a predetermined percentage of profit and as every deposit comes in, immediately take that percentage and put the money away into a 'profit' account.
- In this model what matters is behavior.
- When you ask better questions about your business, you will get better answers. Ask the right questions to reverse engineer your success.
- Taking profit first will force you to break the rules your industry has been following, which in turn will make you the innovative leader.
- More people haven't used this approach as it is uncomfortable. It is far easier to do the processes we are already familiar with.

Parkinson's Law

- This is a behavioral theory. It is human behavior to consume the entirety or vast majority of what is put in front of us. Therefore, supply dictates demand.
- When you take profit first, you will face your business expenses in a completely new way.
- When we have money in our business to pay expenses, we use it all but when you take your profit first, you will become more conservative and innovative in how you run your business.

The Advanced Technique

- Most businesses should have 5 financial accounts.
  1) Income account: All deposits go in here.
  Twice a month take the money in this account and allocate it based upon pre-determined percentages: e.g. 15% profit, 20% owners pay, 15% taxes and 50% to operating expenses.
  2) Profit: Have it accumulate over time, and once a quarter distribute to the owners.
  3) Owners pay:
  4) Tax:
  5) Operating expenses:

Getting Started

- The first step to starting this Profit First process is calling your bank and setting up an additional savings account.
- Nickname your account 'profit' and assign a percentage to it.

Advice

- Expert advice is dangerous, especially when it comes to defining what you will offer your customers.
- The best feedback you will ever get is your customer's wallet.
- The riches are in the niches.

Niches

- A niche is a demographic, which is a definable outward indicator of a person. These indicators are sex, age, marital status.

- A psychographic is a mindset. These are defined by beliefs and feelings about themselves.
- The more often people see you in their target community, the more often they trust you.

Profitability
- If you master profitability, then everything else comes into alignment.
- Flip the formula and don't have profits be the leftover or wait until the end of the year.

Learn more at <u>MikeMichalowicz.com</u>

Take Action!

___ Stop doing actions (Actions you currently do now but should stop doing)

_____

_____

___ Keep doing actions (Actions you currently do now and should keep doing)

_____

_____

___ Start doing actions (Actions you don't do now but should start doing)

_____

_____

___ Who will do new actions? (Assign the action to yourself or someone else)

_____

_____

___ By when? (When will these actions be complete?)

_____

_____

CONVERSATION WITH LARRY WINGET

WHY PEOPLE AREN'T GETTING THE LEVEL OF SUCCESS THEY WANT

CEOWARRIOR.com/podcast-larry-winget/

In this episode of the CEO Warrior Podcast, Mike Agugliaro interviews Larry Winget. Larry is a bestselling author, television personality, social commentator, and internationally acclaimed speaker. He's written over five New York Times bestsellers that have been translated in over 20 languages. Mike and Larry talk about succeeding in business and in life by understanding you are the one who decides what your life is like.

Main Questions Asked:
*   What the hell is the problem with people and why aren't they getting the level of success they want?
*   Where do you see this happening in business?
*   Has social media improved the situation or made it worse?
*   How should somebody get started if they want to take charge of their life?

- If you had a magic wand that could change any one thing in society what would it be?
- What do business owners need to understand about sales?
- What's the best way to build trust?
- How important is it to have credibility and authority in a niche?
- What is something you want entrepreneurs to think about over the next few years?

Mike Agugliaro:	Hello, everybody, and welcome to this episode of the CEO Warrior podcast. My name is Mike Agugliaro and this is the podcast dedicated to the business owners, teaching you how to fast track your business growth and give you practical, doable tips that you can implement today. Grab your pen and notepad and let's get started. Today I'll be interviewing Larry Winget. Let me tell you a little bit about Larry before I bring him on. He's a best selling author, television personality, social commentator, and internationally acclaimed speaker. His newest book Grow a Pair, How to Stop Being a Victim and Take Back Your Life, Your Business and Your Sanity is a New York Times and Wall Street Journal bestseller.

He's also written five additional New York Times, Wall Street Journal bestselling books that have been translated into over 20 languages including Shut Up, Stop Whining and Get a Life, You're Broke Because You Want To Be, It's Called Work For a Reason, People Are Idiots and I can Prove It, and Your Kids Are Your Own Fault. He is also a member of the Speaker Hall Of Fame. Larry has starred in his own television series on A&E, two PBS specials, and two CNBC specials. He's appeared on Dr. Phil, the Today Show, Tool Academy, the Big Idea, Larry King, and in three national television commercials. Larry is a regular contributor on many national television news shows on the topics of success, business, personal finance, parenting, and the wussification of America.

Without any further delay, Larry, how are you, today?

Larry Winget:	I am absolutely amazing. That's such a great introduction I can't wait hear to what I have to say.
Mike Agugliaro:	Yeah, well I'm excited to have you on here. You know, Larry, let's just jump right into this. These are a lot of small business owners listening to this podcast. I would like to hear from you, like what the hell is the problem with people, and why are they not getting to the level of success that they want to?
Larry Winget:	You know that there are a lot of answers to that. First of all, most entrepreneurs should never become entrepreneurs. I know that's contradictory to what most people say. "Just go out there and own your own business, and you'll have lots of freedom, and you'll be in control in your life," which is the most idiotic thing in the world to tell people, because the last thing you have when you become an entrepreneur and own your own business is freedom. You now work for your customers. You work for your employees. You're working your ass off every single minute of every single day.

Most people are not prepared for that, so when they become small business owners and entrepreneurs, and go out on their own and give up their day job, they are not prepared for how much time, commitment, dedication, education that they need, and then they're overwhelmed by what they are facing. They get stuck, and they fall behind. |
| Mike Agugliaro: | Yeah, I see that all the time. For me, Larry, it was like it took me 10 years of pain and punishment to figure out that I had to make a change. When someone comes up to you and says, "You know, Larry, I'm living in business hell." What do you tell them to do? |
| Larry Winget: | Make a choice. Everything is a choice. Everything is your decision. Everything in your life is just the way you want it to be, otherwise, it would be different. So what is causing that business hell? Is it the fact that you have given up control to everything else in your life, all those people that work for you, your customers and so forth, |

or are you in control?

Is it the fact that you don't have any money because your priorities are out of whack, or your spending is out of whack, or you don't understand that customers drive everything and you're not serving them well enough? First of all, it comes down to what your priorities are. You have to do some analysis, and then you have to make some tough decisions.

Mike Agugliaro:	Oh, man, that is so true. Like I watch on Facebook, Larry, and I'm sure as you do. You see these people, and in one post, they're struggling and they're whining, and then on the other post, they just bought a brand new damn boat or something, right, which is just those whole priorities.
Larry Winget:	You know, my post on Facebook, today is that your time, your energy, your money always go to what's important to you. All I got to do is spend five minutes with somebody, tracking their checkbook, their credit card statements, walking through their house, walking through their business, talking to them about how they spend their time, and so forth, and I can tell them what's important to them.
	People are liars. They will say, "Financial security's the most important thing to me," and then they'll do just like what you said, and go out and buy something stupid that they can't afford to impress people that they don't even like. You'll ask them, "What's important to you about your business?" "Well, I want to make sure my business is all of this," and they've got this grandiose, ridiculous, motivated, inspired mission statement, and then they go out and treat their customers like crap, and their employees like crap, and expect to be able to pull that off. That's not how it works.
Mike Agugliaro:	Yeah. Yeah, I can see that. I like what you said, because the important thing is there. Make sure your priorities are in place, and make a damn choice. Now your book, Grow a Pair: How to Stop Being a Victim, you see

people that appear to be victims in how they run their friends, their family, their business. Tell us a little bit about why you wrote that book.

Larry Winget: Well, I write all my books for the same reason. I look around and see what's going on in the world that pisses me off the most, and then I go write about it. That's why I wrote Shut Up, Stop Whining, and Get a Life, which was my first bestseller. I looked at everything that was going on in the financial industry, and people whining and complaining, and I realized that's a parenting issue. Every problem we've got's a parenting issue, so I wrote Your Kids are Your Own Fault, right down the line.

I wrote Grow a Pair because think that we've become this entire society of weenies and wimps and victims. All we do is complain about the problem, and we've lost our ability to know what we believe in, stand up for what we believe in, fight for what we believe in. Really, having a pair, growing a pair, we hear that statement a lot. It's not what's between your legs. It's what's between your ears. People are mentally weak, and they're blaming other people for their situation. I want people to grow a pair, stand up for themselves, figure out what you believe in, and go live it.

Mike Agugliaro: Yeah, that's awesome. Where does this, as you say, "This weenie and wimp stuff," where does it start for people? Did they just wake up and they're there one day? What's your theory on that?

Larry Winget: Well, my theory on that is that's what their mommas and daddies allowed them to get by with. We have ... It's become a popular term right now ... helicopter parents, where parents are trying to save their children from any sort of pain, so they never feel the consequences of their decisions. That's stupid. It's wrong. All you're doing ... I make that absolutely comparable to child abuse, is that when you save your child from ever feeling any pain because of the stupidity of their decisions, then you are abusing them, because we all learn from pain. We learn from consequences. Consequences drive behavior.

When you have an entire society out there that has been saved from ever feeling anything or getting their feelings hurt, then you have all this stupidity we see going on college campuses where people have to run to a safe zone, so that nobody can say anything that hurts their feelings. Then you multiply that by an entire government that wants to step in and take care of everybody all the time. Listen, when you fall down, it ought to hurt. When you reach over and put your hand on a hot burner on a stove, you should get burned. That's how you learn not to do that again.

You know, I base everything I've done for the last 25 plus years in the personal development industry on one of the oldest jokes in the world. A guy goes to the doctor. He says to the doctor, "Doctor, it hurts when I do this." The doctor says, "Well, then don't do that." That's what we've got to get to back in society right now. When it hurts, we learn, "Don't do that again," but we're saving people from hurting.

Mike Agugliaro:	I love it. You got me smiling ear-to-ear here because just yesterday, we were swimming, me and my kids, swimming at the pool. There was this big hornets' nest underneath this umbrella thing, so I was telling my wife, me and my son terminated that thing. She was like, "What if ..." He's 17 years old. He's six foot tall. He's 250 pounds with a full grown beard. She was like, "Well, he could have got stung." I'm like, "He's 17 damn years old. He should get stung," so I love what you're saying.
Larry Winget:	Listen, I got a four year-old, a five year-old, and a two year-old grandson, and I hear their momma out there saying, "Ah, make sure he doesn't step out on the hot pavement when he gets out of the swimming pool," because it was hot, yesterday, 120 degrees. She said, "Make sure he puts on his flip flops first," and all that. I said, "It's a self-correcting problem. When he gets out, he'll say, 'Ooh, that's hot,' and he'll realize, 'When I get out, I should put on my flip flops before I stand on the concrete.' It's a self-correcting problem."

Yet if we save people, as we are prone to do as parents and as a society, right now, save them from everything, we're not helping them. We do that in the name of love. It's not love. It's not love when you save somebody from feeling the pain of their decisions. It's not. It's abuse.

Mike Agugliaro: Yeah, and then Larry, I'm sure you get these ... I don't know if you call them left-wingers where they're like, "Oh, Larry, so are you telling me I should just let my kids run across the highway in traffic?" What do you tell them to something like that?

Larry Winget: "No, I'm not an idiot, and you shouldn't be an idiot, either. There's something called common sense. Use a little common sense." You don't let your kid run out in traffic and get squished and die. You don't prove how stupid you are. Some people are so stupid I'm surprised they can fog a mirror. You use your brain and say, "You know, it's not going to really have long-term effect if he gets out of the swimming pool, and he burns the bottom of his little, tender feet for three seconds." That's no long-term, lasting effect, but it does have a long-term, lasting lesson involved, and so that's what we've got to look at. You can't rob people of the lessons of learning from making stupid choices. You can't do that.

Mike Agugliaro: Yeah, I love what you're saying. My dad used to say, "The problem with common sense is it's not so common." Where do you see this, Larry, falling into business? Where do you see people always ... Maybe the owner's always stepping in, like the micromanager, like never wants people to make a mistake. Have you seen that stuff in business owners?

Larry Winget: Ever fly on an airplane, and you see the last guy to turn off his cell phone because he's talking to employees in the home office and all that, and making sure that everything is done just exactly ... He's the last guy to turn off his phone, and then the instant the plane lands, he's the first guy on his phone, and he's saying, "Well, how did it go while I was on ..." It was an hour flight, and he's so overprotective of what's going on in his business. I see that in all kinds of ways. That's just one of the ways it demonstrates itself.

What that tells me is, one, you're hiring stupid people. Two, you're hiring stupid people, and you're not taking the time to educate them. Three, you are so caught up in your ego that you won't let anybody else do anything, because it's got to be all about you. Four, you don't trust your employees enough to do things. Five, when they do make a mistake, you probably don't use it as a learning opportunity, or you never allow them to make a mistake, so they never get any real experience.

Mike Agugliaro:

Yeah, I could see that. I'm going to ask you a question. I don't know if people have asked this before, but the thing I love about you, besides I could see we've got you all cranked up already, because I feel the same way that you do, is that social media, today, has it improved these problems in situations you're talking about, or has it made them worse?

Larry Winget:

I'm not going to blame social media. I think what social media has done is make us primarily less social, because we don't know how to interact as humans. We don't know how to talk to people. There's also this anonymity of the internet, that I'll never be held responsible for anything that I say, so you see all these people on the internet that have internet balls. They would never think about saying that stuff to you face-to-face. I told a guy the other day, I said, "If you said that face-to-face to me, and called me that kind of thing right to my ... I'd put you on your ass." See the things that we've gotten to is, you can say anything on the internet, because there's no consequences for the internet, so it's made us rude people, incredibly rude. It should never have been called social media. It should have been called unsocial media, so there's that aspect.

The other thing is that we rely so much on technology, right now, that we've forgotten that good customer service, and good leadership, and good management of our people, and good parenting should happen with a

114

conversation. I'm not talking about one you type out in 140 characters. I'm talking about where you look people in the eye, and you speak to them. That's what people enjoy. We've lost that personal touch on a family level, on a business level, on a basic level of just being able to talk to people.

Mike Agugliaro: Yeah. What do you think are going to be the long-term consequence of it. I look at my kids. I have a 14 year-old daughter and a 17 year-old son, and it's like, they're in the living room, which is about five steps away, and they text you, "Hey, Dad, can you go do this?" and I'm like yelling across the room like, "You didn't have to text me. You could have just yelled the damned thing across the room." What do you think are the long-term consequences of this?

Larry Winget: I did a report last week on Fox News about how we see this growing trend among people right now. My report was about the Millennials. We spend so much time relying on technology, that we do back off from one-on-one interactive communications, that people can order all their food online, so they don't have to call anybody. They don't have to go out and eat. They stream everything on their phones or on their laptops or iPads, so we've cut down on the ability to communicate with folks face-to-face.

The long-term effect of that is that I see it's becoming a very hibernated generation moving forward, where we're so cocooned with our device in front of us that we don't know ... I get called old-school all the time, and I say, "Why is it old-school that I know how to have a conversation? Why is it old-school that I know how to when somebody buys something from me, I can count change?" Some of the basics that we have lost ... You know, you pay for things on your phone, and you order things on your phone, and you communicate on your phone. Just like you said, I see families texting each other while they're out to eat, and they're sitting right across the table from each other. You just gave a prime example. You're five feet away from your kids, and they're texting you. We've got to step in as parents and stop that.

Mike Agugliaro:
Yeah. I hope everybody listening to this podcast really hears the message, because I was ... During Father's Day, as I was saying, we got to lead as a different example. My fear, Larry, is that the generation on how ... My father was a mason. He was hard core. On my birthday, he had me out there picking up damned sticks in the front lawn so it looked good. Now, this next generation is being completely lost. One [inaudible 00:17:19] that's on here, How to Stop Being a Victim and Take Back Your Life. Do you have some kind of maybe action item somebody could think about to do this? Because some people are just such a damned mess, they're probably saying, "Okay, Larry, I'm not you. Where the hell do I start? Do I just need someone to punch me in the face, or what has to happen?"

Larry Winget:
You know, I get that a lot. "I'm not you. Not everybody's strong like you, Larry." Well, everybody had the ability to make a few decisions, and to go back and analyze what they really believe in. The first thing I get to in Grow a Pair, the first actual idea is, figure out what you believe, what you will put up with, what you won't put up with. What do you stand for? What are your core values? If I ask people, and I have before ... When I was writing the book, I went out and said, "Tell me five things that you believe in, you'll never compromise on, that if I held a gun to your head, you'd say, 'Nope. That's what I believe in. I'm not giving that up.' Tell me five things you believe in."

When you ask people that, they look at you like a dog looking at a ceiling fan. They don't have a clue what you're talking about, because people have never stopped to examine their core values. I know the things that I stand for and I believe in. My primary thing is honesty. I mean, people don't get to lie to me. You don't get to lie to me. You lie to me one time and I cut you off at the knees, and I'll never talk to you. I'll never do business. We will never have a conversation again. I will not tolerate being lied to. You can tell me the truth, and I don't care how ugly it is, you and I can work with it, as long as you own up, take responsibility to say you're sorry when you need to, say "Listen, I screwed up. Let's move forward." I'll work with you forever. But if you lie to me and deceive me, to hell with you. I'm done. That's one of my core principles I'll never compromise. What are yours?

I got a bunch of those that I feel the very same way about, but when you ask people what they absolutely believe in, their core values ... Core values determine how you run your business, how you run your family, how you run your life. When you are clear about those core values, decision making is very, very easy.

Mike Agugliaro:	Yeah, I love that. It sounds so simple, but it's only simple if you do the action and build them. Even myself, I've never wrote down my personal core values, and so I'm thinking about those right now. That's a great exercise for everybody listening, too. What do you think in today, if you had a magic wand, Larry, and could just change anything in society, people ... I don't care what it is ... what would it be?
Larry Winget:	If I could change people?
Mike Agugliaro:	Well, if you could change anything.
Larry Winget:	If I could change anything in the world, I would roll back to where ... This would be a very simple thing, that I think family time must rule over every other thing that's going on. I think we've got to get back to the fact that families got to eat together at night, and they've got to talk to each other. Again, that will be called old-school. I don't think you ought to have to text your kids to talk to them. I think that we need conversations. I think that parents need to step up and say, "This is what's important to me. This was what I believe should be important to you." They need to let them experience life and feel the pain of their stupidity.

I think that good parenting changes everything in this world, from our financial situation to our political situation, to the housing market and how we treat that, to credit card debt, to student loans. All of that is driven by strong parenting, so I would say if I could change anything, it would be that we've got to get back to being good parents.

Mike Agugliaro: Yeah. I love that, and that is just so true. Again, that sounds easy, but I've even found that myself, you want to wind up the kids and get them for family dinner and one's like, "Ah, I'm doing this," and the other one's doing that. It's funny, because now that I see that my children are getting a little older, sometimes it's a little easier. But now I think they appreciate it. Have you seen it in your own family, and in other families, that once you get it started and the family sees the value and the bond there, that they'll want more of it?

Larry Winget: I believe everything is a habit, and once we establish habits, it becomes an expectation. Habits become expectations, and then expectations becomes just the way we do things. When we establish good habits, and then we expect that to happen on a daily basis, weekly basis, whatever, that just becomes the way you do things. Then that dictates what your life results will be. It works the same way in your business, with your money, everything. "This is how I do things." "Why do you do it?" "Because I expect this to happen as a result of doing it." "And how did you do that?" "Well, I formed the habit of doing it." Just figure out how results happen, and work backwards from that, and let that dictate your behavior.

Mike Agugliaro: Wow. That's really great. Larry, I want to dig into some business fundamental things. You were delivering so many gold nuggets, my fingers are cramped by typing. I love this. Sales. What do people, business owners need to understand about just selling or delivering to customers, today?

Larry Winget: Well, it's always all about value. It's a shame that our businesses have become confused about why they exist, and that our employees are confused about why they've been hire. Employees seem to think that businesses exist to take care of them, to make sure that they are paid enough to fund whatever lifestyle they choose. No, that's not why you've been hired. You've been hired to bring more value to the marketplace than you are being paid. That's why employees need to understand that they should be focused on the value that they bring to the job. The business then needs to understand that they exist for one reason, and one reason only. That is to be profitable. Without profit, you cease to exist, and you no longer get to employ people. You no longer get to pay your suppliers. You must be profitable.

Now how do you become profitable? Well, by offering something of value to your customer, your client, your end user, value. That value must be based on the size of the problem you solve. When you solve a problem, and the only reason you exist is to solve those problems for customers, figure out what problem your solve, and make sure that the customer understands that your solution, your solution has more value than the value of the problem they have. Now see, it's just a very simple equation that we have a tendency to forget.

Businesses must focus. When it's about selling, it's about making sure the client understands that their problem costs them more than your solution does, and you bring that kind of value to the marketplace. Selling is really very, very simple. I was a sales trainer for years and years. Really, it comes down to find out what the customer wants, and give them more of it. Find out what they don't want, and don't give them any of that. Find out what customers want. Find out what problem they have that you have a solution to. Offer it to them. Very simple.

Mike
Agugliaro:

It is so simple, but why is it ... Do you think it's gotten confusing ... I'm curious about this ... because of the abundance of access to information? Like I was telling my son the other day, "Do you realize how we used to get information? It was either the library, or it was an encyclopedia, and when you opened the encyclopedia, you problem coughed on dust or something that came out of it." Do you think that there's almost too much information, that it keeps people from just doing the simplicity, today?

Larry Winget: I think that that's a great excuse. I don't think that there is too much information. I love the abundance of information, and I think that is the most positive side of technology and the internet. I think that we would love to say there's just so much information out there that ... What that does though, is that sort of ties into what I said earlier. Customers are more educated than they've ever been before, so they might know more about your product than you know about your product.

When you look at the fact that ... Look at the real estate industry right now. I saw a stat the other day. It's something like 87% of all houses have been viewed and decided upon online through Zillow and all the other great apps that are out there, before a realtor ever becomes involved. Realtors are no longer needed to show us houses. We've seen the houses we want to buy. What does that mean a realtor needs to do? The realtor must establish a relationship, so they are able to get the listing for the house, and they are able to handle the paperwork that gets them their percentage. It's about the relationship at that point.

Now if all of relationships have been established via technology and online, and via Twitter, and social media, and email, and so forth, we're not going to build that kind of a relationship. The technology has taken away our ability to build the relationship, and the information that's out there means that we're dealing with a more educated customer that doesn't need us to educate them. They can educate themselves. What the client needs us for is to establish a relationship based on trust, so when the transaction must happen, we will still be involved.

120

Mike Agugliaro:	Yeah. That's really good. For trust today, what have you found, from what you talk about, are some of the best ways to deliver or to get someone to trust you?
Larry Winget:	My number one rule for life in business, very simple: just do what you said you would do, when you said you would do it, the way you said you would do it. That's it. Do what you said you would do, when you said you would do it, the way you said you would do it. That's what your customers want from you, and by the way, that's what you want from your customers. Now that also applies to every other area of life. That's why I said it's my number one rule for life and business, is that's kids want from you, and that's what you want from your kids. We all just want that other person, whoever that might be, to do what they said they would do, when they said they would do it, the way they said they would do it. Now that's being honest. That's having integrity, and those things establish trust.
Mike Agugliaro:	Yeah, I like that. That's definitely a simple rule that everybody, I think, would do better, because I mean, I'm sure everybody's had that friend that said, "Hey, I'm going to come and help you on Saturday," and then you're trying to call them, like they're nowhere to be found. Then all the sudden, you're like, "Ah, this guy's just an idiot." You lose trust in him. What do you think, Larry, are some of the ... If you were to give the listeners, "Here's what I would have you think about in the future to create a competitive advantage of some kind in your business." What would you tell them?
Larry Winget:	Well, I would say, do whatever it takes on a social media level, on a personal level, through the way you run your business, that the customer sees you as a resource, not a commodity. I don't care what it is that people are listening to. I don't care what business they're in, I'll guarantee you I can get what you've got from somebody else, probably cheaper. Customers have been driven to the point, it's all about cheap. We've been driven to the point that we're all viewed by most customers as a commodity, so what can you do to move the customer's

mindset from commodity over to someone who is really a resource to them?

That's about establishing value through everything that you do. That's, by the way, how I built an internet following for my business as a speaker and a writer, is that I am daily putting out information that people start to come to me via social media and so forth, to see me as a resource for information. I'm moving out of the commodity level, into establishing my credibility and my expertise, something that sets me apart, they can't get from someone else.

So when somebody's looking ... I don't care if you're running a dry cleaners. Dry cleaning is a commodity. If you can do my shirts for a quarter cheaper, why wouldn't I go to you instead of the guy that's next door to you? Well, you've got to establish relationship. You've got to establish the fact that you could be a real resource to me in making sure my clothes look the best. Anybody could do that in any business, but they've got to start thinking in terms of value, and how do I move from the customer who does business with me, from commodity thinking over into resource thinking?

Mike Agugliaro:

I love that. That is so great, and what a golden nugget there for people to think about, and make sure that they're doing that. Now what about how important today in a business is it for them to have some kind of credibility or authority in their niche or their market?

Larry Winget:

It's absolutely critical. You have to establish your authority. We have a lot of timid people out there ... That goes back to my Grow a Pair book ... who are afraid to talk about what they are able to do. Then we've got the flip side of that, and it's a very dangerous side, about how hyperbole runs the internet, that anybody can say anything grandiose about themselves that they want to, and sadly, there are stupid consumers out there who will believe it. You can say you're the best at something, and probably, you've never done it before, so we have to be very careful about hyperbole, and then we have to be very careful about underestimating our value. We've got both sides of that out there.

So if somebody really wants a competitive edge moving forward, what I would tell them to do is make sure that you capitalize on every resource that you have. Capitalize on the information that you bring, and the tangible benefits you bring to your client base, and really start to make known ... Now that's not bragging if it's fact. You know, there was an old line, "If it's fact, it's not bragging." It's true. If you are really able to do things for people, capitalize on that. Let other people know about that. The best advertisement you have is a happy customer with a big mouth, and the worst advertisement you'll ever have is an unhappy customer with a big mouth.

Now what you have to realize is unhappy customers always have a bigger mouth than happy customers. I've made a living telling bad stories from the stage about people, Radio Shack and the list goes on and on and on. By the way, look what happened to Radio Shack after 25 years of me telling bad stories about them. They're gone. I think I singlehandedly put them out of business. They deserved it, but we have to understand in our business, we are in control of the kind of stories that our customers go away and tell.

Mike
Agugliaro:
Yeah, that's awesome, and I agree with you on the Radio Shack. So what happens today, Larry, people are like, "Oh, I got no time to get things done." You hear this all the time. Time, time, I don't have enough time. What do you tell them?

Larry Winget:
It's what I mentioned awhile ago, that our time goes to what's important to us, and you've got the same amount of time as the average billionaire. It's all in how you choose to use it. If making sure that your customers see you as a valuable resource is important to you, you'll find the time for it. It's sort of the take off on something I heard Zig Ziglar do 30 years ago, that if somebody called you up on Friday night and said, "Listen, I know you got

a big weekend planned. I really do. I know you got to work, and it's going to be tough for you. You've got a big deal on Monday morning, but here's the deal. I just got tickets to the Super Bowl. I got an extra ticket that I'd love to have you accompany me on, but I understand that you're working." Now could you figure out a way to reshuffle your schedule in order to attend the Super Bowl on a free ticket? I'll bet you could.

That's because that, at that moment, became a priority. What you have to do in your life is say, "What is going on that is the most important thing to me?" Once you know what that is, and it's become a very clear priority, let the priorities determine how you spend your time. I'll bet you, you could reshuffle your time that you say you don't have any of, if something was important enough for you to do that.

What I have to do, every single day is ... I'm a busy guy, yet it's amazing now how much free time, Larry time, I've been able to find in my life, because my priorities are so clear. I know clearly what has to be done, not what I'd like to get done. You know, we all get caught up, spending our time, wasting our time, in all the things that we would like to get done. I don't care about any of that stuff. I look at my life every single day and say, "I don't care what has to happen or not happen, at the end of the day, I know this must be done, without equivocation this must be done. I don't care what goes on today, at the end of the day, I have to get this done." When you have that kind of clarity, that kind of clear priorities, and you say, "I don't care if nothing gets done, this has to get done," and then you spend your time making sure that gets done.

Okay, now that's done. Now what's the next most important thing. That's how I run my life. That's how I run my business. If more people did that, they wouldn't get caught up with all the worthless, stupid things out there that eat up their time, that don't really matter at the end of the day. You know, there's nothing more disappointing than finding out you're really good at doing something that didn't need to be done at all. That's where we spend most of our lives.

Mike Agugliaro:	Yeah, that's great. I see it, too, with a lot of my clients and stuff, you see them, they're on Facebook. I mean, you do a post ... I do posts because it's a marketing vehicle ... and they're on there. I'm thinking, why the hell are you on there, right now, when you should be doing something and getting it done. I think that's probably one of the things that social media may be causing a problem with where people are just getting ... I mean, they're taking a crap and they're on there doing that. Do you think that, too?
Larry Winget:	Absolutely. I think it can become a huge time waster, and somehow we work out in our mind that that might be a good thing.
Mike Agugliaro:	Yeah, I'm wondering that myself. They justify it. What is something in one of your books that you wrote, Larry, that you're like, "You know what? Everybody needs to understand this." What's something that just comes to mind right now to you?
Larry Winget:	Well, I read about what it really takes to be successful, and this is a very actionable thing. I love actionable things. If you can't do something with it, it was a waste of everybody's time. I read about the best way to become successful is to get three sheets of paper. Now there's no app for this. Just get three sheets of paper. On the first sheet of paper, write down what your life looks like, your business looks like, your health looks like, your relations. How does your life look right now?

On the second sheet of paper, I want you to write down how you'd like for your life to look in every single one of those areas. If you wrote down that "I weigh 150 pounds," and you'd like to weight 120 pounds, write that down. If you've got this much money, and you'd like to have this much money, write that down. That's what we have to figure out. How is it, and how do you want it to be?

Then, the third sheet of paper is really the critical one. The third sheet of paper is where you write down what you're going to give up to get from where you are to where you want to be. Now that's the most critical one, because we live in a society that is not used to giving up. We have all these motivational bozo idiots out there, who are telling people wrongly, incorrectly, that they can have it all. You've heard them say, "You can have it all." That's stupid. You're going to have to choose.

What my list does is focus on sacrifice. I think I'm the first guy in personal development that went out there and said, "Success comes from sacrifice." So what are you going to give up? We tell people you can get more successful. You don't get more success. You give up what's keeping you from being successful. You don't get skinny. You give up what's making you fat. You don't get rich. You give up what's making you broke. That's it. That's how it works in every single area.

Mike Agugliaro:
I love the part, too, where you said there's not an app for this, because today, you tell someone, "Grab a piece of paper," and they're like, "Oh, is there an app for that?" Yeah, three sheets of damned paper and a pen, and just sitting there and just taking massive action. Have you seen that where everybody's just like, "Oh, man ..." almost if there's not an app. I mean, there might become a point where people won't even know how to use a damn pen no more.

Larry Winget:
Oh, I know. I know. When I tell people to do this exercise, they do get confused. "You mean I actually have to write stuff down?" "Yeah. You have to think about your life. You have to write some things down. You have to figure this out, and you have to give something up." See that's the problem. We've been raised in a society where you never give anything up, so I'm saying, "You can't get more of anything, until you give up some things." People say there's not enough time. Sure there is. There's plenty of time. What are you going to give up to make that time? There's not enough money. Sure there is. Let's go through what you're

126

spending your money on, and figure out what you're going to give up. "Well, I don't want to give up anything."

I had a television show on A&E called Big Spender. I remember, one of the first people I had on there, I was telling her how to get her money back in alignment, and I said, "You've got to give up HBO and all these premium channels." She said, "Well, I'll miss ..." This was years ago. She said, "If I do that, I'll have to give up The Sopranos." "Yeah, you will, but you'll be able to pay for your groceries." "Oh."

Mike Agugliaro:	Oh my god, so crazy.
Larry Winget:	But she was all focused on what she was going to give up, but see, that's where people get stuck. "We don't want to sacrifice. We don't want to give up. We want it all." It can't be done.
Mike Agugliaro:	Yeah, and I see that so much where you tell the people like ... and I find myself repeating myself like, "Wait a minute. If I tell you what it really takes to become successful, will you do it?" I'm sure it's the same with you, Larry, that yes you ... until their blue and they're, "Oh, yeah. I'll do it. I'll do it." Then all of the sudden, they don't want to do the sacrifice. I hear people say it all the time. Like I've been to Anthony Robbins events around so many gurus in the world, and they're like, "I want to be like him." I'm like, "You have no idea what that man, or any successful man that is really doing, today."
Larry Winget:	Yeah, they don't want to go through what I went through to get where I am, I can tell you. I hear that all the time, too. "I want to grow up and be like you." "Well, you want to grow up and go bankrupt, lose all your money, lose your family along the way and have to put all that stuff back together. Do you really want to do that? You want a shortcut to becoming who Larry Winget is. Well, there are no shortcuts." You know, you got to go through the pain. You've got to figure it out.

127

That's what people don't want to do.

I tell you, I charge a lot of money when people want to coach with me, a lot of money. I've had people come in and spend all that money, and I'll say, "Okay, you've got to do this, this, and this," and then they'll want to argue with me about what it takes to be successful. I'll say, "You have no success. You're paying me to help you, and you want to argue with me?" I tell people how to write a best-selling book. Then they tell me, "Well, I don't think that's going to work." "Well, let me see. You've never written a book, and I've written six New York Times, Wall Street Journal bestsellers, and you want to argue with me? You're an idiot. You're too stupid to learn. I'm not giving you a refund, but I'm not working with you. You're too dumb."

Mike Agugliaro:
Oh my god, I could see that, and how that plays out. On the other side, people that are listening to this, I'm such a believer in what Larry just said. You know, if you're going to go and find a coach, a mentor, whatever, like damn, you'd better listen to what they're saying, because they already know. I tell people it's like ... Because I'm doing martial arts, 31 years. Sensei, they call you Sensei. Sensei only means the one who really went before, and I'll add something afterwards. "The one who went before and knows all the stupid shit not to do, again." That's what they need to listen to, so I hear you.

Larry, as we get ready ... We only have time for a couple more questions. What's another big insight that you would like to tell business owners, "In the next two or three years, guys, everybody needs to focus on this." What would it be?

Larry Winget:
I would say it would come down to if you're a business owner, that I would consider you a leader. It's understanding how people are. I see so many leaders wasting their time with losers. Yeah, I am a guy that says there are winners and losers. I don't believe everybody gets a trophy. I don't think everybody has value. They might have value as people, as human beings, but they

don't have value in your business. Some people need to be cut loose, and so I think this is the golden key that if I could give people, it would be to know this.

It's the 20/60/20 rule. 20% of the people are going to be great. 20% of your employees are terrific. They're going to be amazing. They're going to do what you want them to do before you even thought about it. If you didn't show up for the next year, they would do their job and then some. They are that good. Then you've got 20% who are at the bottom. I don't care if you sat there and held their hand and walked them through everything, they're still going to suck. They're horrible. They're not good people. They're not good employees. They're not going to move your company forward. And then you've got 60% in the middle.

What we have a tendency to do as leaders, is spend all of our time with these 20% at the bottom, trying to make them valuable employees, when what we ought to do is once we determine they are never going to get better ... And why aren't they going to get better? They don't want to get any better. They have no desire to get any better. If they wanted to be better, they'd be working on it. If they are working on it, then help them. But these 20%, they don't want to be any better. Cut them loose. Don't spend any time with these people. Forget them.

The top 20%, stay out of their way. The bottom 20%, cut them loose, and then you're left with the 60%. When you're left with that 60%, what you will find is that there is a huge percentage of them just waiting for the space at the bottom, so they can move down there. As your good people, your best people outgrow you and go away, and they will, those people in the middle, some of them have just been waiting for space at the top to step up. What you've got to do with those people in the middle is educate them, train them, nurture those people in the middle to either move up or move down.

It's a constant process, but it's a shame that we've gotten to this place in society that we consider firing people, cutting them loose, saying, "To hell with you. You're not moving me forward. I'm going to release you to a place where your level of desire, and your skill level fits better, because it's not here." We've made that ... It makes you a mean manager, a mean leader if you do that. No, it makes you a good business person. What we've got to do is understand, that's just how employees are. To me, that's the golden key for working with people.

Mike Agugliaro:

Yeah. I feel like you were listening in on one of my meetings on Friday. It was actually during lunch with some of my directors where I told them, I said to my one director like, "Are you being a savior?" because I think that's what he was doing, Larry. He was trying to be a savior. I said, "You just can't save some people."

That's great. Last question. Meetings. What are your thought about meetings. Today, I work with sometimes, I'm in a meeting. I'm in another meeting. I'm in another damned meeting. Just tell me what your theory is on meetings.

Larry Winget:

Some of them are necessary. Most of them are not necessary. Here's what I believe. The best way to have a meeting, stand up. No chairs in the meeting room. Stand up. Meetings will be shorter. Never have a meeting without an agenda. Never. I don't care if it's a meeting of two people. Say, "Look, we are together today to do this, to accomplish this, and here's how I see it going," and then move forward. You don't get together to talk about stuff. You get together to accomplish something, so you must know in advance what needs to be accomplished.

Again, most meetings don't need to be held at all. It could be done with a conversation. Not an email. See, with an email, you can't really emote, except for those stupid little emoticons, which in my opinion, if you have to use an emoticon, it's because you're not able to write a good sentence, but you need the good conversation with people. Pick up the phone and talk to them. Most meetings could be held with just a couple of quick people on a fast conversation.

My last comment about meetings is typically, they involve too many people. Only have the people who are absolutely critical to the end result, the decision making that moves you to the end result. Only involve those. Keep everybody else out of there. The more people you have, the longer it takes.

Mike Agugliaro: I love it. I love it. We had an all company meeting, Larry. It was maybe five, six months ago. We have 180 employees, and there's no chairs. They're used to sitting their ass on a chair. I'll tell you, you would think I'd dropped them off in the rain forest, and like they had no map. It's like the fact that they didn't have a chair to sit their ass in, they were all like [inaudible 00:48:39] confused. That is hilarious, and I agree with you.

Larry, at this point, how do people find out more about you, maybe get books, or just learn more about what Larry has to offer?

Larry Winget: I would say my website is the best place, larrywinget W-I-N-G-E-T, larrywinget.com. You can find me on Facebook, Larry Winget fan page, social media, every place. Because I practice what I preach, I am actively involved on my social media, but Facebook is the chosen one. I don't keep up with all that other stuff. I post one thing and it goes out to every place, so if you just follow me in one place, you're good. But I would say larrywinget.com. You can watch video. You can buy from my store and get any of my books. I've got an online university you can become involved in. I've got an app, very, very simple.

Mike Agugliaro: That's awesome, Larry. Larry, I can't thank you enough for being on today's podcast. I've learned so much from you over the years. I consider you a mentor and a friend. Thank you for being on today's podcast.

Larry Winget: You bet. Thank you for having me.

Mike Agugliaro: Well, there you have it, everybody. I'm going to give you some big Warrior golden nuggets, and I'm going to go fast and furious, so you might need to slow this recording down to get them all, but I'm going to give you some things that really impacted me that Larry has said. Like you need to have a commitment and make a damn choice, right? Make sure your priorities are in place. Don't be a weenie and a wimp. Fight for what you believe in. Lead your family by example, and guess what? Let your kids sometimes feel a little bit of consequences, and use common sense. Don't rob your people from learning from their own mistakes.

Don't hire stupid people, and don't get caught in your own ego. Guess what? Don't just have internet balls. That was really a good, interesting, and fun one for me to think about. Everyone has the ability to make a decision. What are the five things you believe in and would never compromise? I mean, create your own personal core values, and guess what? Get back to damn family time. It matters so much. Sales is about delivering value. Do what you said you would do, when you said you would do it ... Guess what? ... when you said you would do it, right? I mean it's just ... it's so important. It was so simple.

Have your business as a resource for great information in your niche and in your market, today. Capitalize on every resource you have. Man, I told you, fast and furious. What about the simple three sheets of paper exercise, right? What does life look like now? What do you want your perfect life, and what are the action items? The last thing, man, it just hit so home with conversations I was having last week. 20% of your people, guess what? They're great. Stay out of their damned way. 20% at the bottom. They're always going to suck. Don't be a savior. Let them go suck somewhere else. 60% in the middle, and guess what? Spend time, educate and nurture them. And the last thing, guess what? On the meetings, everybody, from this day forward, have stand up meetings.

Well, that's it for this episode of the CEO Warrior podcast. I'd also be grateful if you'd rate my podcast on iTunes. That helps me tremendously with keeping my podcasts visible, so people who have never heard it can discover it. If you have already done this, thank you so much. I'm very grateful. Be sure to connect with me on social media. It's a great way to ask me any questions, or offer feedback on the show. I'm also reachable at mikea@ceowarrior.com.

Until next time, remember, massive wealth and tons of freedom and market domination is only one action step away.

Key Lessons Learned:

People Problems
* Most people are not prepared to become entrepreneurs.
* Everything in your life is a choice, you have the power to decide and change your circumstances.
* Your time, your energy, and your money go to what's important to you.
* Everything is a habit. Habits lead to expectations and that becomes how you do things.
* You have the same amount of time as everyone else, it's about how you use it. Understand your priorities and then let your priorities determine where you spend your time.

Grow a Pair Book
* Larry writes books when he gets angry about what's going on in the world around him.
* Figure out what you believe in and go out and live it.
* Growing a pair is about what is between your ears, becoming mentally strong.
* When parents prevent their children from experiencing the consequences of their actions, children grow up weak and easily offended.
* Non fatal mistakes should be allowed to happen, that's how we learn. Use common sense when it comes to lessons learned.

Business Fundamentals

- Entrepreneurs care about their business to the point that they can't trust their employees to take care of it for them.
- A business is always about value. The business exists to generate a profit by creating value for its customers. Employees should think about their position in terms of how much value they provide to the business, not the other way around.
- Your solution should have more value than the problem your customers have.
- Find out what the customers want, and give them more of it.
- Customers are more educated than ever before.
- Technology has replaced most of what traditional business used to be, it's now about the relationship and trust built between the business and the customer.
- Do whatever it takes to make it so that your customer sees you as a resource instead of a commodity.
- You have to establish your authority in a niche. Be very careful with hyperbole but don't undervalue yourself either.
- The best advertisement you can have is a happy customer with a big mouth. The worst advertisement you can have is an unhappy customer with a big mouth.
- If you're a business owner, you're a leader. You need to understand that 20% of your employees will be great, 20% will be terrible, and 60% will be in the middle. We tend to waste our time on the bottom 20%, don't. Cut them loose, they don't want to learn. Focus on the middle section and nurture them either to the top or bottom 20%. Let your best employees grow and eventually move on. Don't try to save employees that aren't helping you move forward.

Social Media and Technology

- Social media has made us less social.
- The internet has fewer consequences than real life which has made people more rude.
- We are losing our ability to talk to each other face to face effectively.
- Communication technology is replacing actual communication.

- Social media is a tool but it can also be a huge time sink. Don't get distracted.

Your Core Values
- Analyze what you really believe, the things that you believe that you will never compromise on.
- When you are clear on your core values decision making is very easy.
- Core values are things like honestly and integrity.
- Do what you said you would do, when you said you would do it, how you said you would do it. That's how you build trust.
- Honesty and integrity is how you build trust.

Becoming Successful
- It involves three sheets of paper. On the first sheet write what your life, health, and business looks like right now.
- On the second, write what you would like each area to look like.
- On the third, write what you would be willing to give up in order to achieve your goals. You can't have it all, sacrifice what is keeping you from being successful in life.

Meetings
- Don't sit down, standing meetings tend to be shorter.
- Don't go into a meeting without an agenda.
- Most meetings don't need to happen and can be replaced with a conversation, not an email.

Final Tips
- Make sure your priorities are in place.
- Decide what you believe in and stand up for it.
- Let your kids experience the consequences of their actions.
- Sales is about delivering value.
- Don't be a savior for the bottom 20% of your employees, let them go suck elsewhere.

Learn more at LarryWinget.com

Take Action!

___ Stop doing actions (Actions you currently do now but should stop doing)

_____

_____

___ Keep doing actions (Actions you currently do now and should keep doing)

_____

_____

___ Start doing actions (Actions you don't do now but should start doing)

_____

_____

___ Who will do new actions? (Assign the action to yourself or someone else)

_____

_____

___ By when? (When will these actions be complete?)

_____

_____

CONVERSATION WITH DAN KUSCHELL

GROW YOUR BUSINESS AND MAINTAIN A BALANCED LIFE

CEOWARRIOR.com/podcast-dan-kuschell/

In this week's episode of the CEO Warrior Podcast, Mike Augugliaro interviews Dan Kuschell. Dan is a husband, father, and angel investor. Dan started and built 11 companies since 1992, has consulted and appeared on many popular television channels including NBC, Spike TV, History Channel, ESPN and more. Dan and Mike talk about growing your business while maintaining a balanced life.

Main Questions Asked:

* When was the moment you decided you had to set boundaries for yourself?
* What makes the three questions difficult for some people?
* How often should we ask ourselves these questions?
* What are some of the biggest growth dilemmas today?
* What is marketing and how should we think about it?
* What is the one thing that you want business owners to think about over the next few years?

Mike Agugliaro:	Hello and welcome to the CEO Warrior show, my name is Mike Agugliaro and this is the show dedicated to business owners teaching you how to fast track your business growth and give you practical doable tips that you can implement today, so grab your pen and notepad and let's get started. Today I'll be interviewing Dan Kuschell and we're going to be talking about business growth while also maintaining an amazing family life. Let me tell you a little bit about Dan before I bring them on. Dan is a husband, a dad, a serial entrepreneur and an angel investor. Dan has started and built 11 companies, his first in 1992. He got his start in direct mail working with and consulting for health clubs and has been in many radio and TV shows over the years including NBC, Spice TV, History Channel, ESPN and more. He's definitely an expert at helping people build and grow their companies.
	In fact, after selling two of his companies in the late 2000 following a health scare, Dan now spends his time working with fun projects including Joe Polish and Genius Network, and Dan is a servant leader that leads by coaching, driving execution and teamwork, and what that means is you will definitely convert more leads, generate more sales, improve your profits and be able to make a greater impacting contribution. Without any further delay, Dan, how are you today?
Dan Kuschell:	I'm doing awesome, Mike. It's a privilege and an honor to be with you and your CEO Warrior family.
Mike Agugliaro:	I'm excited to have, and why don't you just give us a little insight, like what's happening in Dan's world today?
Dan Kuschell:	What's happened in my world, well I have a simple routine, Mike, because left to my own devices, I'm an addict, I'm a workaholic, I think I've heard Joe Polish refer to it as the respectable addiction so I create a lot of healthy boundaries, rituals to protect myself from myself. I don't know if your listeners can relate to that or I know you and I have had some great conversations together in our Genius Network meetings and for me, I wake up

early in the morning usually between 5 and 6. First thing I do is I get an exercise routine in which I was able to do this morning.

Also, I like to write in my journal and ask question. I find the quality of our questions really determine our destiny, and when we ask better questions, we get better results, and so that's just a solid foundation and basis of what I start my day with, Mike, as well as then seeing my kids off to school and I drop them off at about 7 o'clock this morning at school and then I had it into the office. A big focus right now for us as Genius Network, we have our annual event coming up where we get a chance to serve over 300 to 350 of the top entrepreneurs from all over the world to give them access to connection, access to collaborate, access to high level contributors in the world to really build, grow and accelerate their business to the next level.

My wife and I, the last couple of weeks, we've been spending a lot of personal time, Mike, together and I just had a birthday to celebrate my 47th birthday, so we've got a lot going on but it's been a lot of fun.

Mike Agugliaro: That is awesome and happy birthday. Wish you many more healthy, happy birthdays to come, and so Dan, has it always been this way or there's been some big changes that made you say, "You know what? I better create a routine," and I love what you said, "Protect yourself against yourself." Man, I could just so relate to that, but when was the life change or where the light bulb said, "This got to change, man."

Dan Kuschell: I guess I'm a slow learner, Mike, by nature. I've always been an achievement oriented person. I think it started with sports. As a kid, I thought my way out of this inner city of Detroit which is where I grew up, in the inner city, I thought baseball would be the way, I had career that was developing, and then I fell in love with direct response marketing at a young age, like I was 17 years old when I got introduced to the psychology of how you can put compelling words in print and get people to respond and they would send you money or give you money over the phone or at that time, we were doing it by mail or phone, and now fast forward to today, online.

I've built a lot of these companies and fast forward to the mid-2000's, I was running five companies at once. Like you, Mike, I know with your companies, you have 170 plus employees, I have 175 employees not including virtual team, I was burning the candle at both ends, working about 80 hours a week. I thought I was doing a lot of the right things and I felt we were.

We grew our revenue pretty substantial, we were very profitable and one day, two weeks after my son was born, I have two year old daughter, my son was born, two weeks after he was born, I woke up with chest pains and I end up in a hospital for four days where I had to sign a disclaimer that said I had a one in X chance of dying on the table, and it really kind of freaked me out frankly, because here I was, I don't know how you feel about this, Mike, but if you can remember back being in your 30's, for me I felt like I was invincible, and all of a sudden in one fell swoop, I wake with these pains in my chest, I go to the hospital, the precaution, but then they rushed me into the ... I got diodes everywhere, I mean all chaos just bloody hell's going on all over the place.

They're panicking, I'm panicking, I end up on a gurney, spent four days there and they do this minor procedure and everything ended up being all right, I'm all right today. I'm healthier than I've ever been but that for me, Mike, was the wake up call to really start to identify ... I've got to start doing it different, right? As entrepreneurs, we see things differently. We see opportunities where most people don't. Your listeners, your viewers of what you do, Mike, you instill that behavior and I had that behavior and unfortunately for me, I didn't have complete control of it, and so for me now it's been a quest to really seek out where I can multiply by subtracting, get the biggest impact with the things that I'm doing and then focus on the most important thing and it was that scare back in the late

140

2000's for me that really shifted everything.

I ended up selling two of my companies to take some time off to get my health in order, I've since lost over 60 pounds, I was able to spend a couple of years really as a full time dad, only work on some fun and independent projects and about four years ago, just over four years ago, Joe and I decided to team up to really build Genius Network to another level and it's been a great synergy over the last couple of years.

Mike Agugliaro:	With that being said, if you were to give the listeners which I know, this is a lot of business owners, man, they're burning the light on so many different ends, what would you tell them just to think about and be aware of because Dan, I could tell you for myself, like one of my big scares because I started out being electrician was what happens, I used to say, "What happens if I broke one leg," but I actually tore all the ligaments in an ankle and when you're the business owner, right? If you're still out doing the physical work, like I was on crutches and actually wiring swimming pools because if I didn't work, I didn't get paid, but I mean what happened if I lost both legs? What would you tell people, pay attention to this, everybody. Don't let it catch up.
Dan Kuschell:	There's so many lessons, Mike. One of the things I remember having a conversation or being in a meeting with Joe Polish of Genius Network, because I know you've become good friends with as well, I think Joe said and it may have even been Tim Ferriss at one of the meetings where he said in order to have a breakthrough, you've got to be willing to break something, and also be willing to destroy that which is not excellent, right? Because let's face it, I think a question to ask everybody is when did you realize as an entrepreneur, as you guys are running your service businesses, that you were a little different, right? That maybe you were a little crazy, that you were unique, right? When would be the best time to monetize and optimize what you really know?

We can focus Mike on the transactional side of the

business all day long but what would happen if we really focused on the transformational impact of what our business really can do, right? If we project ourselves out a handful of years and go, "Looking back, what would have to happen in order for me to make the biggest contribution and the biggest impact doing what I'm meant to do in my business," right? That's a great place to start, number one, is asking those questions. For me, after that experience, Mike, I hired a coach and got really ... I've attended, I've figured it out, over 200 events in my career, live events in the personal development industry, in my career, I hired a coach after that incident and I really wanted to get clear for me, more clarity on what made me tick.

Also, believe it or not, I had a self consciousness about me, Mike, where I wondered why I did certain things and why I felt like a black sheep and what I came to realize is being an entrepreneur, that's just normal, but for most of my career, I didn't realize it, but my coach helped me identify that and then these three questions, everything I do today filters through these three questions, and I found them for me to be really impactful and those I've shared it with, they've said, "Wow, those questions are really powerful," and they're really deep too, so the first question I look at asking is what do I want, right? When I went through this incident with my health issue, Mike, I didn't stop and go, "Hey, what did my wife want or what are my kids, what are my 175 employees want?"

What did I want and really start to identify what that is. What am I charged up about? What am I excited? I heard of a recent interview on your show with Keith Yackey and he kind of gave a framework in a little different way around this idea which I thought was really powerful. If you haven't listened to that episode yet with Mike and Keith Yackey, make sure to go do that, but what are your personal talents, capabilities that really fire you up and get you excited and really hone in on what those are? Then likewise, identify what are some of the things that are a drain or a strain on you, that you're frustrated by and list those up, get it clear. That helps you get clarity on what do you want, and then if you had to put a pen and paper, what do I really want to be doing more of in my business and what do I want to be doing less of? That's the first thing.

Second one is who am I, right? Mike, as you know, when you strip away all the titles and revenue and profits and been in this publication, we're just normal people, right? I think I'm probably barely an average person, I'm not superhuman, I don't think I'm smarter than anybody or any better, I've been in business one way or another for over 25 years and the reality is we can lose sight of who we really are, right? We can get caught up in being CEO and we can be caught up in being like this media expert or this author, but take all that stuff away, who are we at our core from a characteristic point of view and identifying who that is, because it'll keep us grounded.

When things go well, there's a mentor of mine, Mike, and I'm sure you've heard this yourself is don't buy into your own [inaudible 00:12:56], right? You've heard that, right?

Mike Agugliaro: Yeah.

Dan Kuschell: Don't buy into your own ... Likewise, don't buy into it when you're high and don't buy into it when you're low, right? If you can stay grounded, the who am I question or who are you question really helps stay grounded, so that's the second one and then number three is what do I stand for, and as you're watching or listening right now to our show and as a part of the CEO Warrior family is what do you stand for, right? These are your values. What are the things that you value most, right? You can do this from a family perspective and a company perspective, like to give a framework, my family, we have the champion values system, like if you ask my kids what are Kuschell values, they'll go, "Champion."

I'll give you the mini version. C is for choose and create, H is for a higher purpose and health, A is for action, being action taker, M is mastery and mentoring, P is purpose, I is invest in yourself, O is being opportunity seeker and N is never quit. I came up with these frameworks around this time, so what do I want, who am I and what do I stand for is a great basis for navigating when the good times are happening as well as when some of the low times are happening but keep us on that even kill to really go out and be a transformational focused entrepreneur, Mike, and really making a bigger impact and contribution.

Mike Agugliaro: Yeah, and I love how the three questions, they're very thought provoking and help you just really understand. If I was to say to you Dan, "Well what makes these three questions difficult for somebody to ask," what would you say?

Dan Kuschell: Try and answer them. That would be the first step. I remember the first time, I mean this process by the way, I still feel it's ongoing because as an entrepreneur, let's face it, we're always evolving the old idea, we're either growing or dying, so we're always, pure nature with entrepreneurs, we're always going to strive to improve, sharpen the ax, get better all the time, grow and go for freedom, and so the first time I sat down with my coach on this by the way, I remember writing one thing down on like what do I want and then staring at the piece of paper with her for about 20, 30 minutes, and that's just where I was at that place and that was about a decade or so ago?

Just taking the time to do the questions, Mike, and trying to answer the question to start with, someone will realize number one, the impact that this will have if you'll stick to it and really be thought provoking to yourself and give yourself this gift to really go do it, and make it part of your personal framework moving forward I would say would be the best way to go about it.

Mike Agugliaro: Yeah. How often do you ask these questions?

Dan Kuschell: Well because of shows like, Mike, and because of the things we do with Genius Network, I find myself talking

144

about them regularly, right? It's like everything we do is conditioning, right? If you're going to get in shape, you don't go to the gym one or two times a year, it's ongoing, you put yourself in a conditioning state, so what I found myself doing is I talk to my kids about this. I'm in conversations like we are today in this. I'm talking to people in Genius Network about these types of things so for me, I put myself in an environment to be conditioning this all the time and it's at the forefront in my journal that I carry with my when I do my writing in the morning, this is part of my process that I'm asking myself regularly and just honing in, refining, continuously updating.

Mike Agugliaro:
I love that. You're around so many entrepreneurs today, business owners on all different levels, what would you say are some of the biggest growth dilemmas for them?

Dan Kuschell:
The biggest growth dilemmas, Mike, I would say, and this is another one I think I originally heard from Joe or maybe Tony Robbins, there's not relationship between being good and getting paid, right? Like you, I met a lot of people, a lot of experts who are really good at the thing they do. They can be good at plumbing, they can be good at electrical, they could be good at customer service, they could be good as a publisher and author, they could be good at speaking but they're not generating revenue and they're not generating profitability or sustainability in their business because there really is no relationship truly to being good and getting paid, and so with that, it's what is the framework to set ourselves up for getting paid, right?

There's a couple that I've learned that for me and for others that I've shared it with have served us well and that one idea is that thinking about the relationship between being good and getting paid, look at a $1 bill versus $100 bill, right? If you get a chance, pull them out, put them next to each other, they're both the same exact size, they're both the same exact weight, the same color ink, there's only one difference between the $1 bill and the $100 bill, and that's the words, the messaging on that piece of paper that makes it more valuable.

When you can become a person who can persuade or influence or market your message or tell your story better at $100 level or $1,000 or $100,000, million dollar level or multimillion dollar level, that's when you'll start to see that when you bring the good talent, combine it with the ability to tell a better story and have a better message, that's when the two exponentially help each other grow overall, right? That's one. The other side of it is a framework around what does it take to build a great business.

For me, I'm a pretty simple guy. Grew up in the inner city of Detroit and I think I look at business in a real simple way, Mike. It's one of the things I appreciate about you as well, I mean all the service you do for your members, all the incredible resources. You're a simplifier and I like to think of myself that way too as a simplifier, so I see there are six key areas of business that when you can incorporate these six key areas in getting working, doesn't mean you have to do them as the owner, right? It doesn't mean that you have to be the expert at it but you just engage people to do these things, these six key areas, you can build something amazing.

In no particular order but I'll say the first two are equally important is marketing, number one, number two is selling or influence, number three is productivity, number four, mindset or emotional mastery, number five is hiring and recruiting, number six is leadership, right? When you can improve, if all of us just worked to improve one percent in those key areas in our companies per week or per month over the next three to five years, what would it do for our business? What would happen as you're listening right now, if you'll improve your ability to market just one percent per week or per month for the next three to five years, what would that do for your company, right? Would you spend more time working on your business versus in the business, right?

You think about some of the blind spots, you think

about the plateaus maybe you're hit with or maybe the overwhelm that you might be facing, well what if you just got one percent better at productivity or one percent better at your team being more engaged with mindset or emotional mastery or leadership, right? Or your ability to sell, so that framework, Mike, I just look real simply at how can we improve in these six key areas of the company and when I go install these in companies or I've installed them in my own companies and been very focused on that, we see exponential results most time because team members also get engaged to want to help grow in those areas too.

What's the old Jim Rohn quote? "We're only going to grow companies to the extent that we grow," right?

Mike Agugliaro: Yeah, I love it. Let's begin, if you're good with it, let's begin to these six a little bit because I think some might feel intuitive by hearing the word but I'm not quite sure it is because if everything was intuitive, well everybody would be exactly probably where they want to be, so let's start with marketing. Give me from your word, Dan, what is marketing today and what should we think about marketing?

Dan Kuschell: Marketing. Marketing is simply telling a better story, right? About what it is that you do and compelling people versus convincing, right? Everybody does marketing, some just do it much better than others, and I look at marketing like field position. Marketing is what you do to get someone either face to face with you or on the phone with you to do business with you predisposed, pre-qualified, pre-interested and pre-motivated one way or another to do business. Selling on the other hand is what you do when you get them on the phone or face to face with you, right? It's like field position, like if you're a football fan and if you're not, just kind of go with the analogy as you're listening right now as a CEO Warrior is when a team kicks off at the beginning of the game or coming out into the second half, if you catch it in the end zone and return it five yards, you've got 95 yards of field position.

147

If you look at that like marketing, that's a lot of work that you've got to do to sell, right? Your marketing took you five yards and now you've got to do a much better job at selling, but if you catch the kick off and return it 60 years, you've only got 40 yards to go. That means you've got better marketing and you've got to be less effective at your ability to sell or influence, so great marketing enhances the salesmanship, right? Also, I learned this from The E-Myth, Michael Gerber, one of the first books I'd got in my late teens or early 20's, he says in that book that "Systems run your business. Find good people to run those systems."

When you can implement and install marketing in your business, you can have average sales people work for you and you can still do way, way above average things, but if you have mediocre marketing, then you're going to need people who at some points in their sales career, going to have to be over zealous, they're going to be closing harder, they're going to be probably be irritating the oyster so to speak from a relationship point of view and five years from now, if you really focus on ... I think traditional marketing, Mike, is actually dead today, and I know that might be counter intuitive. I believe that integrated marketing is where it's going and those who are going to ride the wave of integrated marketing.

In other words, it's not a one time thing, it's not a one time mechanism, it's not one ad, it's not one campaign, it's not one model, it's integrating your messaging, your story with multiple types of pieces. It's like throwing a match at a log, that's the one time thing and thinking you're going to catch a log on fire. I think that model existed maybe five, ten years ago or longer.

Today, it's like taking a piece of paper, you light that piece of paper, you get it burning, then you get some kindling, you put it on top of it, get some little branches, put on top of that, you got a little fire going, you let it burn some more, put some more branches, then you put a big log on top and now you got a camp fire that can go for weeks and weeks and weeks theoretically in the example when it's done right, and that's what integrated marketing, Mike, allows us to do. We don't have to fall in love with tactics so to speak, it's principle based.

I've seen so many people, Mike, and I know you talk about this too, in some of the shows I've heard you do, people that fall in love with the tactics, tactics are temporary but when we really get clear that if principles versus tactics will always win, that's what direct response marketing will give us the ability to do. Tell the better story, to have sustainability for the long term, integrate and also allow us to unwrite, to focus on the relationship value versus the transactional value of our potential clients, customers, shareholders, stakeholders.

Mike Agugliaro: Yeah, and I love that integrated marketing because as much as we would love it to be like throw one thing out and it would just product land flies of clients and customers, it is a different landscape today and you did a great job at explaining that, especially some of the great gold nuggets there about great marketing enhances that sales relationship, so tell me, take me into now, the selling and the things or what you said, influence. I would be curious what is the difference between selling and influence?

Dan Kuschell: I think to me they're the same. A short version definition of selling for me is just helping other people, right? It's providing an adding value, right? It's giving them a transformational opportunity and when we truly know we've got a transformation, as you're listening right now and maybe you're an electrician or maybe you're a plumber or whatever industry service business you're in as part of Mike's family, when you really in your hearts believe in it, you have a moral obligation to share the value of that so that they don't miss out on it, right? People don't want to hire a plumber but what do they want? They want the solution.

They want that toilet unclogged so that they can have a peace of mind and they don't have a stink in their house, right? Or they want the electricity fixed and the wiring fixed in their house with the potential because they don't want their house to burn down because some moron did it incorrectly, right? Did a half-assed job, so for me the definition of selling is simple and influences helping other people get what they deserve as well as adding value. I love Dan Sullivan's definition, Mike, from Strategic Coach who is also a part of Genius Network as you know. He says, "Selling is getting someone intellectually involved in a future result that's good for them so that they will emotionally commit to take action to achieve that result," and I love that because that's good for them, it's good for them so that they commit to take action to achieve that particular result.

That's a side of a way I would describe it, Mike. I think Joe, when you have Joe on one of your recent shows, if you haven't heard of that interview that Mike did with Joe Polish, I'd encourage you to check it out. Joe talked about education based marketing and I think the same holds true in selling today. It's education based selling as well or education based influence and you kind of liken it to a tour. Just like what Joe talked about on the model of an education based marketing idea, he talked about the consumer education guide to carpet cleaning. You could be in plumbing, consumer education guide to plumbing, to cleaning, to restoration, whatever it might be, "Five things you must know before hiring," whatever, fill in the blank overall.

Creating context versus content when you can bring context with content together, it's unlimited to what you can do and then you create a better experience. I mean why, Mike, why does Starbucks sell the amount of coffee that they do at the price they do? It's not because they necessarily make the best coffee, right?

Mike Agugliaro:	Yeah.
Dan Kuschell:	It's because they have a better experience, they take you on a better tour, they're a better tour guide, they're a better experience creator, so all of us, I think one of the keys to marketing and influence today is how can we

become a better experience creator? How can we become a better entertainment creator in the journey of working with us as a business? See, when we can bring experience and some entertainment factor to what we do and how we do it in an authentic way, that's where people, money then is never an issue, it's a measurement of value. Joe even talked about it in the show you guys did. People know I can trust you. I believe there's one other factor that most experts don't talk about besides just no like and trust. It's like and respect you.

See, there's a magic that can happen when you have, call it "The no like and trust" along with respect. Exponentially, you fast forward. Steven Covey alludes to it in his book Speed of Trust. Speed of trust is created when you have respect. Now you can create respect through really good education based marketing and really effective education based influence as well.

Mike Agugliaro: Yeah. Do you think that it's always been education or have we become that education marketing or education based selling is so much more important because people are more careful today? Why do you think the education portion, what makes it different today than 15 years ago?

Dan Kuschell: I would think because 15 years ago, it was probably easier to make a transaction, right? Bad news back then didn't travel as fast as it does today because a lot of the different platforms out there and I think today because of the platforms, I think the companies that do it right, it gives companies a competitive advantage actually if they do it right and really take the time to create a world class experience for their clients or potential clients that they become the only choice in their niche, and I know Mike, you talk a lot about that in what you do. I mean you provide some of the best tools in the world for people that are part of the different programs and resources that you've got available and at the end of the day, I think what people do Mike is they're looking to address two key questions in their head subconsciously.

No particular order, I think those two questions are who

can I trust and how do I feel, right? If you can think through, Dean Graziosi is one of our Genius Network member, he has this whole blueprint idea that he shares with our Genius Network members, if you can start in before unit of your selling or marketing model, before you even get a client and the during unit and then the after unit, you can be thinking, how do they feel at all these different touch points with you, right? How do they feel in the during unit of maybe your tour or if you do an audit in your company to engage them into what it is you offer in your service or the after, after they buy from you, do you have some type of follow up system that's in place to keep them engaged so that you become the only choice overall?

I think those two questions, if we take the time, Mike, to answer, "Okay, who do they trust and why, and what can I do to be their trusted authority," and number two, how do they feel and then work to supply the solution to making sure that you're giving them the best feeling that they can get versus any of the competitors out there, that's when we have the chance to win.

Mike Agugliaro:	Yeah. That's awesome, and I would say listeners are getting how powerful it's like. I think it's more than just saying "Ask a better question." You need to know the question to ask but then asking and really digging deep into it. Talk to us about productivity. Isn't it productivity, life productivity, just what you feel about people should know about productivity in general?
Dan Kuschell:	Yeah, I think the easiest way I could describe productivity, and we can go deep in all of these, Mike, and I'd certainly love to is what's the most productive, I think I learned this originally from one of my original coaches, Brian Tracy, what's the most important thing that I can do in every given moment? Then the second question is what's the most important thing can my team be doing at every given moment, right? One of the things that I've worked really hard and I think because of my influence with the E-Myth back in my late teens, early 20's is I looked at marketing and selling as the

linchpin, Mike, and what I mean by that, as you guys are listening to this as well, what if you could go out there and you could, because let's face it, where do you waste probably most of your time in your business as far as the selling?

Is it prospecting or is it enrolling or closing sales? Chances are most business owners are spending most of their times having a prospect for new business, right? Most businesses operate, they spend 50, 60, 70, 80% of their time doing prospecting and only about 20% asking for the sale or the enrollment, however you want to, whatever your framework is in your model. What if you could actually create a model that allow you to spend 80 to 90 to 95% of your time enrolling versus, and you had a marketing system that could supply you the prospects?

To me, being productive, doing the most important thing at every given moment is how can I create a sales model or a marketing model that can allow us and our team and our team members or our team members to actually be in a position where they get to enroll or they get the ability to ask for the sale, 80, 90, almost 100% of their time, let them spend the time doing what they're best at and then you can have other people doing some of the other things to kind of feel like you certainly have someone who's going to be required to service people who might be required to handle inquiries, someone who might be handling some of the follow up and communication, some of the publishing that you might do, the education awareness guides, those sorts of things.

I think it starts with the question "What's the most important thing I can do in every given moment? What's the most important thing could my team be doing in every given moment," and then likely start with the marketing and selling system that you've got in work from there.

Mike Agugliaro:	That's like such gold there just to ask that question not only of yourself, what's the most important thing I can do at every given moment. I think that's one of those

things where you probably say to yourself, "Well maybe Facebook or watching TV, maybe that's not the most important thing at that point," so I appreciate you letting us crank through these things because I think the deeper dive just makes it so much helpful. I know you can probably spend a darn day or more on each one of these but take us through mindset, but I'm curious about the mindset. Go ahead.

Dan Kuschell:
Yeah, and Mike, going back to even productivity. Look, I don't claim to have figured any of these out myself, right? I'm on a journey as well in working to get better systems and all of things and when you get conscious of them, and like I shared, my improvement in the last ten years because of just being focused probably positions me just a little different, like I am so grateful and thankful I've got a system for productivity of managing email. I've got less than 20 emails in my inbox right now, right? Because I have an assistant who filters them for me and I trained her in how to filter them and setup certain patterns, rituals of how she can respond versus not.

Is it perfect? No, it's certainly not perfect but I'll tell you, having the freedom, having the peace of mind that I'm not caught up in the business of responding the email two or three hours a day versus now it's probably less than 30 minutes a day total, I mean what would that do for some, just that one little strategy if someone could install it? It's the old idea, Mike, of little hinges can swing big doors. It makes such a big difference all the way around, so you started to hit on mindset before I cut you off and I apologize.

Mike Agugliaro:
Yeah, no, that was great that you shared that because I think people, they're not seeing the little things they're doing that are sucking a lot of time when you add it up because they're like, "Oh, it's just a minute here, a minute there," and the part about the email, people have to be opened up. There's a world. You could have somebody on the other side of the planet that's checking your email. It's not anymore where you need a full time employee

154

and they have to be on insurance and they got to have an office to sit at and a desk, like there's virtual people that can do that, but yeah, the mindset, so mindset in general, I'd like to hear about mindset of business growth. Tell me where's the blocks on this.

Dan Kuschell:

I think a couple angles for that, Mike. The mindset starts from a business perspective, what business are you in, right? A lot of people think they're in a certain business and I would challenge that thinking, like if you think you're in the plumbing business or the electrician business or whatever service business that you think you're in, well what if you slightly adjusted that, and I know, Mike, you speak to this as well really well, what if you looked at ... I'm actually in the marketing of the business I'm in, right? The old Peter Drucker quote is "Business has two functions, marketing and innovation. Everything else is a cost," right?

I've heard Dan Sullivan, Mike, in Genius Network say marketing, innovation and teamwork, everything else is a cost, right? Because let's face it, you can leverage your growth through better marketing/innovation and teamwork with a great team. You can also of course make the worse mistakes you've ever made by hiring the wrong people or having the wrong team or doing the wrong marketing, that sort of thing, so I think it starts with what business are you and maybe looking at your business a little differently that what if you were in the marketing of the business we're in, what would that do for you? The other part is so many of us I think fall in love, Mike, from a mindset.

There's scarcity based mindset and there's abundance and prosperity based mindset. Scarcity says there's a limited amount, abundance says "Let's make the pipe bigger," and as you're listening, and I don't claim to have figured this out myself, I'm fortunate enough in Genius Network, we have about 250 current active members in the community, I was the third member in Genius Network when Joe started it back in 2007, I met hundreds and hundreds of top entrepreneurs in the

155

world. From people like Richard Branson all down to a guy like me who was in Genius. How they even let me in the community, I'm not even sure, but nonetheless it's the idea that there's scarcity and not enough to go and I have to hold on to my personal ideas and my personal agendas and my personal frameworks.

What I've discovered is the higher up you go, the more contribution you're willing to make to others regardless, and I love this quote from Disney because I think Disney was revolutionary in the way he looked at entertainment for families and kids and business, and I read one of his biographies and one quote that always sticks with me, Mike, is this quote. He says, "You can steal the idea but you can't ever steal the magic," right?

Mike Agugliaro:	I like that.
Dan Kuschell:	Yeah, and all of us have our magic and our businesses, don't we? As you're watching or listening right now, you have your magic, so even a guy down the street who might be the same industry, the same service, the same type of thing, you have your magic that's different. The key is what are you going to do to accelerate that magic? What are you going to do to make it better? Disney didn't look at he was in the amusement park business, he looked at it as he was in the entertainment business, and what could he do to create a better experience that people couldn't get anywhere else from him, and that also goes to another framework around this mindset of scarcity versus abundance.

Abundance mindset says focus on ten times growth or exponential growth. Scarcity mindset says I'll focus on incremental growth, I'll focus on the transaction today, I'll focus on the 10% growth I need to make in my company this year, so it's that ten times growth versus the 10% growth mindset, Mike that I think I see and I've met, I know you have two in Genius Network that really paid dividends, right? The most expensive information is that information, but so often, we want to price ourselves to be the cheapest, right? We want to price ourselves so that we're competitive, right? Because of scarcity in most cases. Well what if you could go out and create an experience mixed with some entertainment because of your magic that you could charge two to three to five times more than everybody else in your industry? What would that do for you?

If you just raised your prices 20% because you said, "You know what, even if I lose 20% of my customers but I increase my price as 20%," you realize most of you, depending on your business model and your prices, would actually increase your revenue and your profits significantly. That's a mindset shift, it's one of the simplest things that all of us can do in our business is looking at how can we increase our prices by simply adding either value that we didn't already have or actually starting to articulate going back to messaging the $1 bill or it's our messaging telling a better story of going, "Oh, you probably didn't know we already do this and have this value to what we do but let me make you aware of it," and now that they're aware of it, they go, "Oh, you're the best choice in town, right?"

Those are a handful of the things, Mike. I also see mindset personally as a leader, as an owner, as an entrepreneur that we all are, perhaps as a family person because as much as I like to integrate and talk about business, I also really pride myself on now being able to integrate this with my kids, my family and it's just the way of life, but I look at the mindset or the whole person that we are in six key areas. It's mental, it's physical, social, spiritual, emotional, and financial, and usually when you get the first five, mental, physical, social, spiritual, emotional in check, the finances will actually come and it seems like a counter intuitive thing but I see this happen all the time.

Going back to my one percent improvement model in the business focus, what if you work to improve yourself mentally just 1% a day? Maybe it was a personal development, maybe it was investing in Mike's programs, maybe it was investing by going once a year to Mike's training or a couple of times a year depending on where you're at, mentally improving, physically, like I've lost over 60 pounds, Mike, and I've capped it off. I'm just under 10% body fat today. Now I'm 47 years old as you know, it isn't as easy today as it was when were in our 30's or 20's or whatever, but that takes a commitment, but I look to improve 1% physically by integrating different types of training. Yoga, meditation, and more, so physically, what could you do to improve 1%?

Spiritually, whatever your belief system might be, I like to believe there's a higher power out there. Now I happen to be a Christian personally. Whatever your beliefs are, take mine out of the way, whatever your beliefs are, what if you worked to improve just 1% spiritually, right? On a monthly, weekly, annual basis? What would that do on an annual basis I should say? Mental, physical, spiritual, social. If you're like me, I'm actually more of a quiet, shy, introverted type of person, and Mike, you and I talked about this, and what if you got out of your comfort zone and made a commitment to, I know Joe Polish talked about writing five cards a day five days a week, 25 plus per week as far as the relationship building. I don't even go simpler than that.

What if you just did that with one per day? Just one card extra day or made a commitment to make one extra commitment to a contact, to meet somebody you hadn't met before, one per day? What would that do for you, right? Mental, physical, social, spiritual, emotional, right? There's all kinds of courses, emotional intelligence has become a hot topic. I won't spend a lot of time on emotional intelligence or the concept, but really starting to have empathy and feeling what that is, you can see through our clients and see through our client's emotions and we can speak to that with authenticity, man, there's no limit to what we can do because we create a great connection with people.

Then financially, what can you do to improve financial? There's so many world class experts in finance, and again, I know Mike, you bring a lot of these resources to improve these areas so the beauty is you're part of a CEO Warrior family, you've got access to get improvement in all these areas, so that would be a few of the frameworks, Mike, that I look at and there's certainly more but I think I'll stop there now.

Mike Agugliaro: Yeah, that's really incredible information and the thing that kept the in and out to me, Dan, that most people probably don't realize is they spend so much time thinking, and they might need it, "Hey, I need marketing and I need sales profits," and it goes back to that mindset thing you're saying. If you just improved your own personal mindset 1%, well you would be able to see the different marketing, see the different sales, see different opportunities, so that's great. I like to close out on these next two, if you could just touch slightly on them, hiring and recruiting. What's your beliefs on, you've hired so many employees, and then close that up with your beliefs in leadership.

Dan Kuschell: Absolutely. For hiring and recruiting, Mike, I mean again, we could go much deeper on it but hiring and recruiting I see as a marketing system as well, and the unfortunate part for a lot of us as business owners, like selling, like maybe not having great marketing in our businesses at times, and I'll just speak to me, I won't speak to anybody else. I know in my 11, the reason I've had 11 companies, part of that is I've had some shit ton of failures along the way, right? I've learned from my mistake but I found that when I put a marketing system in place for hiring, and yes, I've actually interviewed over 22,000 people in my career, I've had over I think 5,000 people work with me either as an independent contractors or employees, and today, I love to have a marketing system around hiring.

Think about all the time that it takes to interview, right? We want the great talent on our team, we know that talent can help us, it can leverage us, it can grow us, but the cost, the opportunity cost of taking the time to hire can be expensive and I get it, so what if you put up a marketing system in place to help you with your hiring, something as simple as running an ad that drives somebody to an entrepreneurial survey that maybe has some of your company core values built into it that they have to respond to? That would be step one and if they didn't fill out that entrepreneurial survey, first of all, you're finding out if they can pay attention to directions, you can see if they are articulate in how they write, if that's a requirement in whatever role you'd have them in.

If it's a sales position, one of the things, Mike, I had regularly done, I've got a little noisy here, I apologize. One of the things that I've regularly done is put people in a position to do the thing that they're actually going to do. I remember years ago for selling, we used to have people respond to our ad and they'd leave a voice mail message telling us why they'd be an ideal candidate, and if they were somewhat articulate and had something going on, Mike, I had an admin.

I didn't even do this near the end of that particular company, she would call them back and she would just say to them, "I was following up, I got your message, interested. Tell me a little bit more," and then she would go, some version of this, you'd go, "I'm not really feeling it, I'm just not sure you'd be a right fit," and so if that salesperson candidate bailed out, right? Well we knew we didn't have a good fit, and if they look to overcome the objection and sell her on why they would be a good fit, well as long as they weren't a complete overbearing maniac and egomaniac with it, well then she would schedule them to come in and review, so you can create a little marketing systems like this.

Today, like even in Genius Network, we put out an entire model and I'll give you a simple one to think about, Mike, that your viewers and listeners at CEO Warrior can adapt. Run an ad for whatever position to an entrepreneurial type survey. Once they fill out the survey, if they met that criteria in your mind, then ask them to submit a video to you outlining why they would be a good candidate for your company. Now if they send you a response that's, "Oh, I don't have the camera," just say, "Well you have a phone so just shoot a quick video on your phone and email it over," right? It doesn't have to be high production value, you want to make it super easy for them to understand what the parameters are, you're just looking to get a feel would they be a right fit for you, and you could save so much time.

First of all, you'll have a percentage of people that won't do the video which means they're not up on technology, they're probably not going to represent you as an A player in some way, done well and done right, and if they do do the video, you're going to have a chance to pre-screen them before you and/or one of your team would actually ever schedule an official interview. Now let's say they do the entrepreneurial survey, let's say they send you a video, they meet the criteria. What do you do next? I recommend doing a Skype interview where possible, right? Skype is free, it's easy to use, you can do a Skype call and/or a Skype video with them and have a video chat. I like using the video chat because it just works well to see somebody eyeball to eyeball and make contact and you can spend ten minutes.

This is about efficiency, it's about effectiveness and it's having that marketing system and usually what we would do is based on that interview, we would give them some kind of a mini assignment to do relevant to the kind of work they might be doing for us. If it was an admin person, we might have them go listen to Mike Agugliaro's podcast and do a summary of it to give us an idea how they write content and how accurate they are with their grammar in selling. If they were a salesperson, we would do something different, but think of what you would want that person to do for you and then put them through a process basically a marketing system to do it.

Hiring is a marketing function, Mike, and done well, it's not a cost of time or money, it becomes an accelerator and elevator, a multiplier to help grow, and think about it. What would it be worth for you to spend more time on your business versus in it? I have a virtual personal assistant that handles my email. I've got less than 15 emails in my inbox right now. It hasn't always been this way. There have been times, maybe like as you're listening right now, I've had thousands of emails and felt buried and overwhelmed, even as little as like 6 months ago and I finally had enough and I said, "I've got to get it done." I made a commitment, I hired somebody, I trained her, I took the time and it's been such a blessing to be able to now spend more free time focused on things that matter, that make a difference, the bigger contribution, the bigger impact for the company for our client.

Being able to spend time like this with Mike and you, so I challenge you, think of how you can build your marketing system there in hiring and recruiting, and then leadership, Mike, I'll leave with one quote and it's an adaptation of the Forrest Gump quote. Leadership is as leadership does. Don't listen to what we say, watch what we do, and our team would do the same thing so lead by example. That's the simplest, shortest version I could give you based on time.

Mike Agugliaro:	Yeah. I like that, the "Don't watch what we say, watch what we do," and I think it says it all right there when you think about it. Okay, Dan, last huge question because man, me and you could just go forever on this stuff.
Dan Kuschell:	Yeah.
Mike Agugliaro:	Let's say you step out, we got a million entrepreneurs, you step out on whatever, the largest stage or above the whole whatever city or something and you get to tell them something they should really think about over the next one to three years, what would you tell them?
Dan Kuschell:	Wow. That's a really great question. I would say focus on this question. Three years from now, what would have to happen for you to have a greater contribution and impact? If you start focusing on what the answers are to that question, there will be no limit to what you can achieve. It will allow you to be a transformational type business, a transformational type leader versus a

transactional one. You'll be able to focus on more of relationships versus transactions. See, people don't cancel or refund relationships. Joe say that over and over again. People do not refund or cancel relationships, so if you can put yourself in a position on what is the impact, what is the contribution, what is the ten times growth? You want to build a ten million dollar company? What's the hundred million dollar problem you got to solve in your community?

If you want to build just a million dollar company, what's the ten million dollar problem you got to solve? It's a ten times impact. What is your ten times impact, what is your ten times contribution that you're committed to be able to make, and focus on that. I would even go back to the three questions we hit on earlier, Mike. What do you want? Who are you? What do you stand for?

A couple of great questions that one of our Genius Network members shared with us recently, Alex Charfen at charfen.com. It's what is my intention for today and what was I uncomfortable with yesterday, and then what can I do about it today, right? Powerful questions. A couple of questions that I ask my kids regularly, usually over dinner conversation or before bedtime, a handful of questions, what am I grateful for right now? What am I happy about right now? What have I done well today? What mistakes did I make and what did I learn from it?

What's amazing, Mike, the more I think we focus on what do we have to be grateful for, the more we will have to be grateful for. The more we focus on what we're happy about, the more we will be happy about. The more we focus on what we've done well, the more good things, great things, incredible exponential things we'll actually accomplish, and yeah, I think those are a good framework to start with. There's certainly more but that's a good place to wrap.

Mike
Agugliaro:

Wow, yeah, you got me over here. My brain is like running wild thinking about all this stuff. How did people, Dan, at this point, they're like, "Where is this guy, Dan? How do I find out more about him?" How do they do that?

Dan Kuschell:	First of all, I'll say Mike, one of the best things people can do is you provide so many valuable resources, I want to encourage you to go deeper with Mike's got available for you with all the tools, the resources and so on. As far as being able to reach out to me, you can find me at Genius Network here with Joe Polish, with the community that we've been building. You can email me at dan@joepolish.com. If there's anything I can help you with or our community can help you with, please feel free to reach out. Additionally, I've got a radio show weekly here in Phoenix that also syndicates nationwide. You can go check that out at growthtofreedom.com, that's growthtofreedom.com.
Mike Agugliaro:	That's awesome. Dan, I can't thank you enough. I'm honored to call you a friend and a mentor and I so appreciate you being on today's show.
Dan Kuschell:	It's been a pleasure, Mike, thank you, buddy.
Mike Agugliaro:	There you have it, everybody, and I'm going to go through some gold nuggets back but I am never going to make it through all of the gold nuggets on this one but let's just crank through as many as I can do right now, so protect yourself against yourself. Holy mackerel, that was just such a big highlight for me, and guess what? Ask better questions, get better results. In order to have a breakthrough, sometimes you need to destroy something. Three big questions that Dan mentioned, right? What do I really want? What excites you and who am I and what do I stand for? What do you value most?

No relationship between being good and getting paid, right? Tell your story, then the rest with a stronger message, and then man, did he lock and load us on the six key areas of business to improve? Marketing, selling, productivity, mindset, hiring, leadership, and he told us about marketing, right? Great marketing enhances the sales relationship, right? Then he went into selling an |

influence, right? Help other people by adding value. People want a solution and he did an amazing job talking about education based selling, and what about productivity, right? What is the most important thing I can do at every given moment? Now that's part one. Part two, what can your team do right at every given moment? That's the most important thing.

What about the mindset, right? What business are you in? What mindset do you have? Do you have a scarcity or abundance? Hiring and recruiting, right? Guess what? It's a marketing function and he gave us some cool ideas on how to make that so much better, and leadership? Guess what? Leadership is as leadership does. Don't watch what we say, watch what we do, and then he just tied a big ribbon around this thing, three years from now, what would have to happen for you to have a greater contribution and impact? What a powerful episode.

Well that's it for this episode of the CEO Warrior show. I'd also be grateful if you'd rate my podcast on iTunes. That helps tremendously, would keep my podcast visible so people who have never heard it can discover it. If you've already done this, thank you so much, I'm very grateful. Be sure to connect with me on social media, great way to ask many questions or offer feedback. I'm also reachable at mikea@ceowarrior.com. Until next time, remember, massive wealth, tons of freedom and market domination is only action step away.

Key Lessons Learned:

Setting Boundaries

* Being an entrepreneur can be stressful. Many people sacrifice their health and their lifestyle in order to be successful in business.
* Focus on the activities that drive the most results rather than trying to do everything yourself.
* Get clear on the answers to three questions: what you want, who you are, and what you stand for.

Growing a Business

- If you want a breakthrough you have to be willing to break something.
- There is no relationship between being good and getting paid.
- Being able to market your message is how you get paid.
- There are six key areas of business:
- Marketing, Selling/Influence, Productivity, Mindset, Hiring and Recruiting, Leadership.
- Improving just 1% each week or month can lead to incredible results.
- People don't refund relationships.

The CHAMPION Framework

C – Choose.
H – Higher purpose and health.
A – Be an action taker.
M – Mastery and mentoring.
P – Purpose
I – Invest in yourself.
O – Be an opportunity seeker.
N – Never quit.

Marketing and Selling

- Marketing is simply telling people a better story about what you do.
- Marketing is what happens before you get someone face to face. Selling is what happens during the face to face.
- Marketing enhances the sales process, they complement each other. Weak marketing means your selling ability has to be better, great marketing makes the sales process easier.
- Integrated marketing is the future, a single campaign isn't as effective as building momentum.
- Selling is the process of getting someone committed to a future result that will be good for them.
- Seek to become a better experience creator. Customers don't buy your services, they buy the results and the experience.

Productivity
* Ask two questions: "What is the most important thing I can be doing at any given moment?" and "What is the most important thing my team can be doing?"
* Start with your marketing and selling system and optimize that so you can focus on more important activities.
* Systems are important to being able to focus.

Mindset
* Is your mindset one of abundance or scarcity?
* Do you try improve your business or yourself every day?

Hiring and Recruiting
* Hiring is an extension of your marketing system.
* Put the prospective employee in a position to test them for what you need.
* Having a few filters in the system will make the selection process easier and faster, people will self select and opt out leaving the more qualified people.

Leadership
* Lead by example.

Final Tips
* Ask better questions to get better results.
* Tell your story better than your competition.
* What is the most important thing you can be doing at this moment.
* Leadership is as leadership does.
* How can you create the greatest impact?

Learn more at GrowthToFreedom.com

Take Action!

___ Stop doing actions (Actions you currently do now but should stop doing)

_____

_____

___ Keep doing actions (Actions you currently do now and should keep doing)

_____

_____

___ Start doing actions (Actions you don't do now but should start doing)

_____

_____

___ Who will do new actions? (Assign the action to yourself or someone else)

_____

_____

___ By when? (When will these actions be complete?)

_____

_____

BONUS INSIGHT

BREAKING DOWN LIMITING BELIEFS

Limiting Beliefs Are Holding You Back From Success And Higher Achievement, Use This Strategy To Help You Break Through And Finally Achieve Your Goals

Imagine struggling for a decade – working 24/7 and very nearly broke. What would you do in that situation?

That's exactly the situation that my business partner and I faced in the in the first decade of our service business. We almost had to shut the business down! But something changed and we ended up turning things around and building up a business that now makes more than $30 million a year.

Not surprisingly, the question we're often asked is, "WHAT CHANGED?"

The Surprising Turning Point In My Business

People want to know what that one turning point was that really got the ship turned and headed in the right direction.

Well, certainly there were several factors like our education and mentors, an investment into ourselves, a focus on building the right kind of business, and more.

But the biggest change happened the moment Rob and I said, "Maybe we don't have to shut the business down. Maybe we can fix it."

That might seem like a small thing to you but I can tell you it was PROFOUND. That was the turning point when we DECIDED that there was an option and we BELIEVED that we had a different way that would work for us.

You see, for the first ten years of our business, having only seen other struggling service companies working a certain way, we had formed a set of beliefs about our business and how it should be run. Those beliefs included:

169

- Business should be hard
- You should struggle; it shouldn't be easy
- You need to work 24/7
- You shouldn't enjoy your work
- Success takes a long, long time
- Your business comes first and everything else (including family) comes second

Those were our unconscious beliefs about our business. They were shaped by what we observed about other businesses and those beliefs determined how we viewed our own business (and it obviously also impacted our lives).

Beliefs Shape You

That's what beliefs do. They determine the shape of your business and life. Positive beliefs create a positive and successful and expansive business and life; negative beliefs create a negative, struggling, and restrictive business and life.

Think of your life as if it were a house… the walls and roof are your beliefs. Those beliefs determine the shape and size of your house. Negative beliefs will create a small, dark, closed-in house; positive beliefs can create a huge, expansive, bright, and welcoming house.

I like what Henry Ford has to day about this: "Whether you think you can, or you think you can't – you're right."

He's talking about beliefs. Your belief that you can do something will allow you to do it; your belief that you can't do something will keep you from doing it. In my service business, the first decade was a struggle because I didn't think my business could be any different; later, I changed my belief and suddenly expanded my business.

What Are Your "Walls"?

You have beliefs about everything. From business to relationships, from religion to money, from politics to health, from how you spend your free time to what you eat for breakfast in the morning… EVERYTHING we do in life is determined by our beliefs.

Most of these beliefs are created very early in life, often from family and teachers (and sometimes from friends and the media). A couple classic examples include:

Our parents' relationship with each other will usually set up a series of beliefs for us about our relationships with future partners – either we'll want to emulate our parents, or we'll want to be the opposite of our parents, but most likely their relationship will in some way unconsciously guide and inform ours.

Our parents' and teachers' instructions about money will often get us to think about money in a specific way for years to come – for example, we're often told as children that money doesn't grow on trees. (I disagree with this and specifically explain why in my book The Secrets of Business Mastery.)

Once these are created, they unconsciously guide us daily, just as the walls of your house silently create the shape of your home without you giving them a second thought.

And for most people, they live their lives with these beliefs – often LIMITING beliefs – that keep them from living the life they want to live.

In fact, many people end up frustrated, broke, struggling, and even angry because they aren't living the life they want to live and they don't know why (and they don't even realize that it's all because they have beliefs in their heads from when they were young that are causing them to think this way.)

Break Down Those Walls

What if you could change the walls of your house? What would you do? Probably you'd break them down and then build – build up and build out for a bigger, more expansive house.

The same thing is true for your beliefs. You do not have to live with these limiting beliefs! Instead, you can change your thinking and start living a life that is as positive, successful, and expansive as you want… and achieve the same kind of turnaround and transformation in your life and business that Rob and I saw when we changed our beliefs about our business!

It starts by stating what your limiting beliefs are. (This is hard because we don't always know what they are – but work at it and think about the beliefs you have about certain things.)

Example: it took Rob and I a while to figure out what our limiting beliefs were about our business… but we finally did!

171

Once you've stated a limiting belief, DESTROY IT. Seriously, just shred it. (That's what we do at my Warrior Fast Track Academy events in one of the most powerful exercises we do!)

Example: Rob and I decided that we weren't going to struggle in business anymore.

Then, create a new belief. A powerful, positive, expansive belief that replaces the old one. (Hint: you have to truly BELIEVE this with every single cell in your body.)

Example: Rob and I decided that we had the power and could get the knowledge to turn things around.

And, you'll also need to support it and take action on it.

Example: Rob and I invested in our education and constantly took action to apply that education.

Do This Daily

Our entire lives are determined by our beliefs and, while many of them are positive (or at least well-intentioned) MANY of our beliefs limit us. Make it a daily exercise to destroy your limiting beliefs and create better enabling and empowering beliefs for a more powerful "Warrior Life".

Break down those walls daily and expand the house of your life.

As Henry For told us, "Whether you think you can, or you think you can't – you're right."

… so maybe it's time to start thinking that you can.

SPECIAL REPORT:
NETWORKING YOUR WAY TO BROKE

HERE'S HOW SERVICE BUSINESS OWNERS FIND THE ONE INDUSTRY GROUP THAT WILL ACTUALLY MAKE A MEASURABLE DIFFERENCE TO THEIR BUSINESS' GROWTH... INSTEAD OF THROWING MONEY AWAY AT HIGH-COST, LOW-VALUE MEMBERSHIPS

This report is for service business owners – including plumbers, HVAC, and electricians – who understand the importance that an industry organization or group can play in the growth of their business.

If you are either currently <u>looking for an industry organization or group to join</u> or are <u>disappointed by the results you're (not) getting from the organization you currently belong to</u>, then make sure you read this report all the way through because you may be surprised by what you learn...

You're on a journey and you reach a fork in the road. But not just two potential paths... Rather, you have a dozen or more potential paths. Each path *promises* to help you get to your preferred destination but when you look at the dejected faces of people traveling in the opposite direction, you know that not every path will do what it promises.

Welcome to the world of home service industry organizations and groups. There are many available and each one promises to train you to grow your service business with the latest strategies and industry best practices, to provide networking opportunities, and perhaps discounts on marketing or services.

Unfortunately, **many service business owners learn the hard way that these organizations are not delivering on their promise; instead, they happily accept your hard-earned money for their expensive memberships but rarely deliver back the value you hope to get.**

Year after year you promise yourself, *this year I'll dig deeper to get more out of the group*, or, *this year I'll try a different group*, but you get to the end of every year and discover that nothing has changed. **Your money has been wasted.** (And yet, if you're like most service business owners, you continue in the organization because you hope that next year will bring you the value you need.")

The results speak for themselves: you might take away a half-decent idea now and then, or you might benefit from the occasional group call… but you have a hard time justifying the membership cost.

Forget the empty promises of training and networking that will once again fall through.

What do service business owners really want? If you're like most service business owners out there, you probably want **practical ideas that you can implement immediately to get fast results**; and, to be frank, **you might even benefit from the occasional get-your-ass-in-gear push to help you overcome the frustrations and obstacles that plague you daily**.

Use this list to diagnose whether you're wasting your money at your current industry organization or group, and to see what option will actually create positive measurable growth in your business.

#1. Are The Owners "In The Trenches" Every Day?

Some industry organizations and groups are run by people who haven't run a home service business in years; others are run by people who have never worked a single day in the home service industry!

CEO Warrior is owned by Mike Agugliaro and Rob Zadotti, who previously owned Gold Medal Service and grew it to become New Jersey's #1 home service business, employing 190 staff, serving 125,000 customers, and earning more than $30 million/year. After selling the company, Mike and Rob continue to work closely in the home service industry and are always learning and testing to share only the strategies that have proven to work.

Would you rather hear from someone who is no longer in the business or someone who is still in the business daily?

#2. Have The Owners Of Your Industry Organization Discovered The Path To Success?

Many industry organizations simply pass down their best practices from one generation to the next, and those who run the organization just "parrot" what they've heard before. *If* they're in the industry, they're just moderately successful… or perhaps have merely *inherited* their thriving home service business rather than built it up from scratch.

Mike and Rob started out as electricians. For the first decade of their business the two of them worked 24/7 and struggled to make ends meet. After nearly burning out and shutting the business down they decided to fix what was broken, so they invested heavily in their own education then rebuilt the business from the ground up. The next eleven years were completely different, with year-over-year growth of more than a million dollars annually.

Would you rather get "hearsay advice" that is parroted from a previously successful person, or learn the strategies and systems from the same person who struggled then figured it out?

#3. Do the Owners Invest Heavily In Education?

If you currently belong to an industry organization or group, find out what the owners have learned recently. Ask them. Do they have a growing knowledgebase of current field-tested strategies that they've culled from the best-of-the-best?

CEO Warrior does! Mike and Rob have invested more than $1,000,000 into their education and have studied the best strategies even from organizations outside of the home service industry. Disney, Zappos, Amazon, Nordstrom, Joe Polish, and others – CEO Warrior mines the best strategies from these best-of-the-best companies.

Do you prefer stale strategies that have not been updated in years or the latest field-tested ideas inspired by the world's best-of-breed companies?

#4. Does The Industry Organization Have A Million Dollar Guarantee?

When you attend an industry event, what kind of guarantee do they have? Many don't offer any kind of guarantee; at best, you might hear the vague "If you're not satisfied, we'll try to make it right" promise.

CEO Warrior's 4-day Warrior Fast Track Academy events come with an iron-clad $1 million dollar guarantee that promises: "***If you get to the end of the very first day and you haven't learned enough strategies that will make you an extra million dollars or save you a million dollars, then simply ask for a refund and you'll get 100% of your tuition, PLUS the cost of airfare and hotel to get to the event, on the spot... no questions asked.***"

What's the guarantee of the industry event you attend?

#5. Does The Industry Organization Provide Swipe-And-Deploy Marketing Templates?

Many home service business owners fiercely protect their marketing and will never share it. That same thinking is carried over into industry organizations where you might (but probably won't) get "plain vanilla" marketing ideas that may or may not work.

CEO Warrior is different, though. You get a binder that is literally stuffed with marketing templates that are actually being used right now in the marketplace, bringing in millions of dollars of business monthly for home services businesses all over the world. When you receive these marketing templates at a 4-day Warrior Fast Track Academy event, you have permission to modify and use in your own business – and you'll even be introduced to the name of the printer who can print them for you!

In your current industry group, were you handed a big swipe file and introduced to the exact people who were able to deploy it for you?

#6. Does The Industry Organization Feel Like A Brotherhood?

When you attend an industry event at your organization, what does it feel like? Do you nod silently to the other attendee before stealing a quick glance at their name tag because you can't remember who they are? You barely remember anyone's names because you just don't engage with these people enough.

At CEO Warrior, you may join the CEO Warrior Circle, which is a tight-knit brotherhood of service business owners. You'll be on a first-name basis and think of these other men and women as more than just colleagues – but as friends, family, and fellow "Warriors" as you fight together to grow your service businesses. CEO Warrior Circle members become a family and will do ANYTHING for each other, supporting each other professionally and personally.

When was the last time you felt like you were part of a close-knit brotherhood that cared about your success?

#7. Are You Just Paying For Friendships?

In most organizations, you're paying that expensive membership fee for what – a few friendships that you might or might not value outside of the networking event?

At CEO Warrior, you'll make solid friendships with other CEO Warrior Circle members but the real value of the group is the life-changing results that can transform your business and deliver more wealth, freedom, and market domination. You'll be connected to a strong group of fellow Warriors, each of whom is highly interested in your success. You'll make friends, yes, but you'll discover that the CEO Warrior Circle is all about helping you grow your business to create the business and life that you want.

Wouldn't you rather invest in yourself and your business than for expensive friendships?

#8. Do The Large Companies Just Promote Themselves?

In many industry organizations and groups, you'll encounter business owners of all sizes… And usually the small guys will chase around the big guys and try to find out what their secrets are (only to have the big guys simply promote themselves without ever sharing good ideas.)

CEO Warrior Circle is not about self-promotion but about everyone pulling together so that everyone can win. Each Warrior steps up and is willing to help the others. **What kind of brotherhood is CEO Warrior Circle? You could probably call any of them in the middle of the night for an emergency and they'd be there for you. Could you do that in your current industry organization or group?**

Would you rather hear a big company talk about themselves or a successful company share their best ideas with you?

#9. How Long Do You Have To Wait To Get Support?

One frustration that you may have with your industry organization is how long you have to wait to hear back from someone, especially if you're looking for help or advice. Maybe they only respond during business hours, or maybe they promise a 48 hour window to reply.

Mike and the CEO Warrior team are very responsive – **offering insight and advice in social posts, live video, email, and text messages at just about any time of day or night.** They recognize how important the Warriors are and they strive to serve them.

Would you rather wait hours (or days) to get help, or get help right away?

#10. Does Your Organization Take A One-Size-Fits-All Approach?

Nothing is more frustrating than getting some useful-sounding strategies… only to discover that these strategies only work in a business that is different than yours. Maybe you run a rural business but the ideas only work in town; maybe you have a team of 5 but the ideas only work if you have a team of 100.

CEO Warrior serves businesses of all sizes, in all locations. No matter how your business is configured, the strategies and guidance you'll receive will be custom-tailored to fit YOUR unique situation. There are Warriors all over the world – every size of business in many different markets. The strategies you get will work in your situation. Period.

Would you rather hear general advice that might not apply to you or the best field-tested strategies that will work in your specific situation?

#11. Is There An Emphasis On Growing Your Business Or Growing Your Life?

The last time you were at an organization or group event, how much emphasis was placed on your life? Probably very little. Most industry organizations try to help you grow your business – that's their purpose. Problem is, they don't care where you get the time and energy to make the necessary changes.

At CEO Warrior, the emphasis is on growing your business so that you can have the life you want. You'll learn the strategies to grow your business and you'll also discover how a healthy family life can help your business (and vice versa). You'll even hear how to stay healthy through the life and lifestyle of a service business owner.

Why grow your business at the expense of your family when you can have both – a successful business and a fulfilling family life?

#12. Does Your Group Tell You The Honest Truth, Even If It Hurts?

Most of us want to hear nice things – but if you're reading this then you're smart enough to know that a hurtful truth is better than a comforting lie. Yet, how often does your industry organization or group say something harsh but necessary? (Hint: they probably won't because they want you to renew your membership!)

Mike Agugliaro is known for his no holds barred, no BS approach. If a Warrior needs to hear something, Mike will say it. The honest truth, even if occasionally hurtful, is far more advantageous to hear. And, it's not just an honest truth told *to* you, there's also ongoing accountability to "hold your feet to the fire" to help you do what you say you're going to do.

If you'd rather be lied to, then join some other group. But wouldn't you rather hear the truth if it benefits you?

#13. Does Your Group "Nickel-And-Dime" You For Different Services?

In a lot of industry groups and organizations, members pay a membership fee to get access to a few things, and then they're expected to pay extra for additional products and services (like events and extra coaching).

CEO Warrior Circle members enjoy an all-inclusive experience where unlimited coaching, events, and resources are included as part of the membership investment. You simply won't get another bill for needing extra help.

Does your current group or organization care more about the fee or about you?

#14. Do You Get To Learn Directly From The Guru, Or Are You Pushed Off On Some Trainer-For-Hire?

Maybe this has happened to you: you pay your membership fee and you look forward to hearing from the guru or main person behind the group… until you actually start to interact with the group and you find out that you're stuck with a trainer-for-hire working out of a call center who follows a script and references the same resources you received when you first joined.

CEO Warrior Circle members get full access to Mike and Rob—experts who are in the industry daily. Whether by phone, text, or email (as well as webinars and events), you'll interact with the same gurus who started CEO Warrior Circle.

When was the last time you heard from the guru in your group?

#15. Do You Learn Cutting Edge Internet Marketing Strategies?

A lot of groups teach generic marketing strategies with little, if any, internet marketing. And many groups that do teach internet marketing are teaching things that worked for them 5, 10, and even 15 years ago.

CEO Warrior Circle members get the latest cutting edge internet marketing strategies that work right now for service businesses – and the reason these work is because they're being constantly tested and refined.

How current are the internet strategies you've learned? (Have you learned any? Are they currently being used?)

#16. Do They Share A Lot Of Information For Free?

Most industry groups will make a lot of promises about what you'll get when you join and force you to pay thousands of dollars to actually access the information. Very few will even give you a little glimpse into what you can learn, forcing you to put up a lot of money to find see if they're for real.

At CEO Warrior, you can learn so many strategies for free – whether by books, social media (Facebook, LinkedIn, and Twitter), or CEOWARRIOR.com, Mike shares many of his best ideas and strategies. In fact, one person watched Mike's free videos and applies his strategies over a 2-year period and increased the number of techs in his business from six to 20. And, many more business owners see even bigger results faster by attending Mike's 4-day Warrior Fast Track Academy

Could you more-than-triple your workforce from the free information provided by your industry group

#17. Do You Get A Free 30 Minute Strategy Session To Even See If This Is The Right Fit For You?

Most industry organizations and groups will tell you to pay if you want to find out whether it's right for you or not. You risk your money and time without really knowing until it's too late whether the information you're learn is helpful. Perhaps they throw some generic ideas at you in an attempt to wow you but they're just regurgitating the same information for everyone.

At CEO Warrior, no one can attend the Warrior Fast Track Academy without first getting a free 30 minute strategy session. These strategy sessions are FOR you and ABOUT the strategy, problem, question, challenge, or opportunity of YOUR choosing. Simply share the struggle you want help with and the CEO Warrior expert will work with you – for free – before you can even attend the Warrior Fast Track Academy.

When was the last time you got a 30 minute free personal one-on-one strategy session with your industry organization before they even allowed you to move forward with them?

#18. Are There Events That Your Family Wants To Attend (That Actually Help Your Family Members Understand What You Do?

Most industry events are technical and boring. Your family begs not to go, and they don't really care what you learn while you're there. But wouldn't it be nice if they could attend to understand what you do? And wouldn't it be amazing if they had such a good time that they begged to go back again?

CEO Warrior Circle members often bring their spouses to events – from regular Circle events to special Warrior Relationship events, your spouse will love the event and will have a better understanding of what you do so they can support you as you grow your business.

When was the last time you attended an event with your spouse… and your spouse asked to go back again?

#19. Do You Dread Those BORING Live Events?

Most industry events are a bore! Look around the room and you'll see people trying to stay awake while the speaker drones on and on. You keep checking your watch. You drain your coffee cup and can't wait for a break to refill it. You spend more time checking your phone for messages than you do watching another boring PowerPoint slide presentation.

CEO Warrior events, including the Warrior Fast Track Academy, are anything but boring. Audiences are captivated by Mike's style, by his strategies, and by his level of service that he brings to every presentation. Some CEO Warrior Circle events even include firewalking! Make sure you get a good night's sleep before the event because you'll be "on" the entire time, and you'll leave with a level of inspiration and energy you didn't think was possible!

When was the last time you actually were excited about attending an industry event?

#20. Do You Leave The Live Event With A Road Map Of Success?

Many people attend industry events with the hope of getting a couple of good ideas that they can bring back to their company (and sometimes they'll even remember to implement those ideas when they get back!)

But those who attend Mike Agugliaro's Warrior Fast Track Academy events get something different: you'll work WITH Mike throughout the 4-day event to create your own customized 90 Day Road Map that outlines the step-by-step strategies you want to implement in your business to grow in the next 90 days. And by the end of the event, Mike and his team will even check your Road Map to make sure it's clear and achievable so you can start implementing it immediately. (Some attendees even start implementing before they leave the event.)

When was the last time you left an industry event with a multi-million dollar step-by-step Road Map to implement in the next 90 days?

The choice is yours – will you continue paying for an industry group or organization that…

… doesn't deliver what it promises?

… takes your money and then asks for more?

… feels like an expensive way to meet a few other friends in the industry?

… is difficult to reach anybody when you need real help?

… doesn't share the best, most effective field-tested strategies and ideas?

… run by people who aren't in the industry?

… doesn't seem to care about your business (or your family)?

Or, will you finally step and realize that YOU and YOUR BUSINESS (and YOUR FAMILY) are worth making the switch to a group like CEO Warrior – a true brotherhood of like-minded business owners who want help each other, led by an industry leader who will always be there for you?

The very first step to learn more about how CEO Warrior is different is to attend the 4-day Warrior Fast Track Academy – to learn more, to get many of the benefits described above, and to see if the CEO Warrior Circle is right for you.

Go to <u>WarriorFastTrackAcademy.com</u> to apply.

Are you tired of treading water – staying busy in your business but never really getting ahead? **Are you ready to discover the most powerful strategies to create real change, growth, and market domination in your business?**

Whether you're new and totally overwhelmed or you're a seasoned pro and looking for to reignite, The **Warrior Fast Track Academy** can show you how to get to the next level.

Warrior Fast Track Academy is my 4-day hands-on event where I guide you and a group of like-minded service business owners through the exact plan that I used to build a $30+ million (and growing) business. I'll reveal the blueprint and show you how you can implement the same blueprint into your business, with all areas of mastery planned out and ready to be plugged in. You'll be motivated and inspired to lead positive, profitable change in your company and take your business to never-before-seen heights.

Business owners who have attended the Warrior Fast Track Academy have said it's "life changing" and gone on to build successful businesses all around the world.

If you want to take control of your business and your future, Warrior Fast Track Academy is THE event to make that happen. To see what others are saying about Warrior Fast Track Academy, to learn more about my $1 million guarantee, and to pre-register for an upcoming event, go to **WarriorFastTrackAcademy.com**

"You are the average of the 5 people you spend the most time with."
(Jim Rohn)

... Who are YOU spending time with?

Here's the fastest way to leverage the power of proximity by spending time with like-minded action-takers who work together – to grow your business while striving to become unstoppable.

Most industry groups and organizations take your money and give you just a few stale best practices and networking opportunities. But at CEO Warrior, we've created **a powerful, exclusive "family of Warriors" who discover the best secrets and field-tested strategies, and who hold each other accountable while implementing them.**

Welcome to the **exclusive, invitation-only CEO Warrior Circle** where business owners can join to become Warriors and inspiring leaders of a strong and growing business.

During the upcoming year, we'll revolutionize your business and your life. We'll blow your wealth, freedom and personal goals out of the water by focusing on massive business building and life strategies. From weekly calls to exclusive events, from one-on-one coaching to an exclusive vault of swipe-and-deploy resources, joining the CEO Warrior Circle gives you everything you need to grow your business.

This program is designed for action-takers who are ready to make the commitment and take action to boost their business.

To learn more about the Warrior Circle, and to see if you qualify to participate in the Mastermind, get in touch at
CEOWARRIOR.com/contact

READ THE FREE MAGAZINE WRITTEN FOR THE HOME SERVICE INDUSTRY

Discover new information, insight, and industry-specific success stories in Home ServiceMAX – the free online magazine written for home service business owners.

Each issue of Home ServiceMAX is packed with practical tips and strategies that you can implement right away into your home service business. They're field-tested and written by experts and industry insiders.

Home ServiceMAX will help you improve your sales, marketing, finance, human resources and customer service. Keep it on hand as you develop best practices to meet your team's unique challenges.

Whether you're a plumber, electrician, carpenter, roofer, builder, painter or specialist in any other service industry trade, to survive you must also stand out as a business leader. We designed this magazine to help you achieve that goal.

Each easy-to-read issue is available online for free. Check out the articles and make sure you have a pen and paper in hand to write down all the actions you'll want to take when you're done each article.

Read the current issue and subscribe here: HomeServiceMaxMag.com

ABOUT THE AUTHOR

Mike Agugliaro, Business Warrior

Mike Agugliaro helps his clients grow their service businesses utilizing his $30 Million Warrior Fast Track Academy Blueprint, which teaches them how to achieve massive wealth and market domination.

Two decades ago he founded Gold Medal Electric with his business partner Rob. After nearly burning out, he and Rob made a change: they developed a powerful blueprint that grew the company. Together, Mike and Rob grew Gold Medal Service into the top service industry provider in Central New Jersey. With over 190 staff and 140+ trucks on the road, Gold Medal Service. Before selling the company, it was earning over $30 million in revenue each year.

Mike is a transformer who helps service business owners and other entrepreneurs master themselves and their businesses, take control of their dreams and choices, and accelerate their life and business growth to new heights. Mike is the author of the popular book The Secrets Of Business

Mastery, in which he reveals 12 areas that all service business owners need to master.

Mike speaks and transforms around the world; his Warrior Fast Track Academy events are popular, transformational events for service business owners; he also leads a mastermind of business owners known as Warrior Circle. Mike has been featured in MSNBC, Financial Times, MoneyShow, CEO World, and more.

Mike is an avid martial artist who has studied karate, weaponry, jujitsu, and has even developed his own martial art and teaches it to others. The discipline of martial arts equips him to see and act on opportunities, create change in himself and others, and see that change through to successful completion.

Mike is a licensed electrician and electrical inspector, he is a certified Master Fire Walk Instructor, certified professional speaker, and a licensed practitioner of Neuro-Linguistic Programming (NLP).

Whether firewalking, breaking arrows on his neck, studying martial arts, transforming businesses, or running his own business, Mike Augugliaro leads by powerful example and is changing the lives and businesses of service business owners everywhere.

Mike lives in New Jersey with his wife and two children.

IN THE MEDIA

An article published in the HVACR Business Magazine discussing the struggles of being a service business owner and sharing his Situation Analysis Tool to help make better business decisions.

READ

ceowarrior.com/hvacr

This article is about strategies to build a strong and productive team. This is one of many articles that Mike has published through Comfortech.

READ

ceowarrior.com/contractor

Featured in a TV segment on the Nightly Business Report on CNBC. This interview shares how Mike, as an electrician, started his own business and is now advising other entrepreneurs how to be a CEO Warrior in their business.

WATCH

ceowarrior.com/cnbc

CEOWORLD MAGAZINE

Mike shares 5 powerful mindset shifts to rapidly grow your business. These are some that helped him grow his $28M business.

READ

ceowarrior.com/ceoworld

IN THE MEDIA

Mike shares tips on how to motivate your staff by discovering their why. It's a strategy he uses to leverage and motivate his staff of 190 with great success.

READ

ceowarrior.com/thenews

Vendors are a great resource – and Mike explains why. He explains how you should choose your vendors to create stronger and more lucrative relationships and partnerships. This article was also published in Entrepreneur!

WATCH

ceowarrior.com/foxnews

MSNBC interviews Mike Agugliaro and business partner Rob Zadotti to share how they grew their service business from $1M a year to over $28M one employee at a time, through processes and systems.

READ

ceowarrior.com/msnbc

CEO Warrior Owner Mike Agugliaro Hosts Fast Track CEO Workshop, Sept. 13-16

CBS8 featured an article about Mike, CEO Warrior and the 4 Day Warrior Fast Track Academy and how it helps service business owners.

READ

ceowarrior.com/cbs8

The Secrets Of Business Mastery: Build Wealth, Freedom and Market Domination For Your Service Business in 12 Months or Less. A chapter-by-chapter collection of best business practices, tools and strategies for service business owners.

Secrets of Leadership Mastery: 22 Powerful Keys To Unlock Your Team's Potential and Get Better Results: 22 powerful keys to help you create a culture where you build and lead a hardworking team of superstars, inspire them to give their very best, and generate measurable results.

Secrets of Communication Mastery: 18 Laser Focused Tactics To Communicate More Effectively. We all communicate. We can all learn to communicate more effectively. When you do, you'll see instant results in every personal and professional relationship.

Timeless Secrets of A Warrior. Discover the most powerful, time-tested Warrior secrets that will propel you toward success by revealing strategies from some of history's greatest minds.

9 Pillars Of Business Mastery Program: Discover the nine most powerful and transformative strategies that are PROVEN to completely transform your business and your life.

YOUR BUSINESS SUCKS!

(Or maybe it just feels that way!)

Perhaps your business is wearing you down every single day and you're thinking about shutting it down and going to work for someone else instead, just because it's easier.

Perhaps it's going okay (maybe it even feels successful) but you've hit a plateau and you can't quite break through – so it sucks because the higher level of success eludes you.

Here's the good news: your business doesn't have to suck. In fact, with just a few changes, you can unlock strong, rapid growth that completely changes the game for you:

- Earn more money and keep more of it as profit
- Hire A players and build a strong culture where everyone loves to give their best
- Finally start generating real leads that turn into happy customers
- Build a business that runs on autopilot – so you have more time to spend with family

If you own a business that is not delivering more of these things to you daily then this book is for you. You'll discover the strategies and secrets you need to finally create a successful, fulfilling, meaningful business for you.

Get the book on Amazon or at:

CEOWARRIOR.com/books/whyyourbusinesssucks

CONNECT WITH MIKE AGUGLIARO

Connect with Mike in the following places and find even more free resources and strategies to help you grow your business.

Website: **CEOWARRIOR.com** – Go here now to get free resources, including chapters from Mike's book and a library of resources.

Warrior App: **CEOWARRIOR.com/warriorapp** – stay up-to-date on the latest strategies and events by downloading the Warrior App for iOS and Android.

CEO Warrior World Facebook Group: **CEOWarriorWorld.com** (forwards to the Facebook group; you can also search on Facebook for "CEO Warrior World")—discover powerful secrets and connect with other business owners as you learn from Mike and share your own triumphs in business.

Podcast: **CEOWARRIOR.com/podcast**

Events: **CEOWARRIOR.com/events**

Social: Visit **CEOWARRIOR.com** to connect with Mike on Facebook, Twitter, LinkedIn, and elsewhere.

Home ServiceMAX Magazine: **HomeServiceMaxMag.com**